THE ZEN SIDE OF BUSINESS OWNERSHIP

HOW TO BE TRUE TO YOURSELF IN EVERY PRODUCT YOU DELIVER.

ERIC URIARTE

To Jonathan.

Find your mission!

Eric Uriarte

G1 DESIGN LLC

Cover Illustration: G1 Design LLC

To the dreamers, the innovators, to those who dared to start a business, create jobs, and support communities around them. The world thanks you for following your lofty ambitions and striving to be the best at your craft.

CONTENTS

PREFACE

Zen : a state of calm attentiveness in which one's actions are guided by intuition rather than by conscious effort 朿

What drew you to this book? Are you an entrepreneur considering starting a business or an owner looking for ways to jumpstart your company? Are you currently contemplating countless business concepts and opinions about marketing, forecasting, streamlining and culture? Are you researching slues of experts offering their perfect formulas for success? Unfortunately this is where many entrepreneurs find themselves. Not exactly a Zen business owning experience.

If you are in the formative years of creating your business, faced with getting things off the ground, you may find that success is nearly impossible just from the list of start up "requirements" alone. Maybe your current business just needs that one big deal or a few higher top line targets to set you on the right track. Then everything would be perfect – everything would be Zen? But would it?

Seasoned business owners know that it doesn't matter how much money your business brings in if it can't sustain profitability. Let's take a look at that from a different perspective. For a little fun, we'll use a car as a metaphor for your business. An automobile is a great tool for getting from point A to point B, assuming that the car has all four wheels, a working engine, seats and all the accouterments needed to stay comfortable on your long journey. Would you ever, as a consumer, accept a car that came with only one of these crucial features? For instance, just the seats? Of course not. Yet we easily slip into the trap of thinking about business as just top-line sales. It's like saying that the only thing that matters is the number of seats in your new car. Wouldn't you agree that it's better to have a more economical vehicle with all the components fitted and working perfectly than to have a larger, more luxurious SUV with comfortable leather seats but no wheels?

Let's say your business is growing, you are making a profit, but something is amiss. Everyone feels like a sell-out. Your staff never goes the extra mile for your customers and no one knows the true heart of your business. An environment like this most often leads to customer turnover, burnout, downsizing, disputes...the lot. Which would you prefer? Getting to your destination slow and steady or the alternative, not getting there at all? Is it better to have a lower grossing, more efficient, profitable, and ethically run business or one with a huge top line that's operating at a loss? A car with no wheels cannot drive far. Success comes from understanding your business from a perspective that includes much more than just the sales column. This is the beginning of a Zen approach to your business.

So what defines true Zen business ownership? I offer the following answer: ZEN BUSINESS OWNERSHIP IS...

An enterprise that:
1) truly embodies you *H-gc.!*
2) is profitable
3) creates a following of supporters
4) serves a community

All four of these elements are required to get you to the Zen Side of Business Ownership. Adopt only three and you'll find yourself struggling with the business in some regard. Is it possible to get to your destination without the front windshield of our metaphorical car? Yes, but you'll most likely arrive with bugs in your teeth. Similarly, can you run a business that lines your pockets but doesn't truly embody you? You can, but the true Zen Side of Business Ownership will remain just out of reach. You will be missing out on something universal to the core of most every entrepreneur - sharing the very portion of your business that is you and creating meaningful connections with the community you serve.

With all your searching for the right answers, is it possible that the solutions to your business challenges have been under your nose this whole time? Is it possible that you already know everything you need to run a successful business? Is it possible that you were born with the very talents and qualities you need in order to succeed? I'm proposing you do. But how do I know?

I've learned and earned the knowledge that we have all that we need within ourselves. Years spent in business seminars, studying business curriculum, voraciously reading through business, self-improvement materials, and following experts with endless lists of to-dos has taught me this very important fact. Creating visions and growth plans targeted to one-up my competition, I've even talked smack to prove that I was better than my competitors. By playing the price wars I've won some sales. I said "yes" when I should have said "no" just to keep people from going to the shop next door. To keep my customers coming back, I've cut corners to stay profitable and promised cheaper deals.

But in reality this wasn't me. Becoming a corner cutter was not in my business plan. It wasn't my style to tear down others to succeed. I was not a turn and burn person. What happened? Another me had taken over in the process of trying to grow a successful organization. I felt like a sell-out. I felt threatened every day. The one-way relationship I had with my customers grew tiresome and I anticipated the day they would leave me for a better deal. I hated my business ownership experience.

Customers can generally spot a phony and when I finally realized that I was not being true to myself, I vowed that I would never "sell out" again. Deep down, I really wanted a following of supporters who understood me, understood my mission and would be willing to get behind it. Customers who would pay to help me achieve something bigger than me. But who was I, just someone with dreams of being the best in my craft. My business was comprised of a hodgepodge of ideas and trends at best. I needed to rebuild my business in a way that reflected my goal of excellence. Mine would be an organization that could deliver; one that people could get behind.

Starting with a clean sheet of paper, I made notes on myself. It was a deep dive into what drove me; what drove my creation of a business and what mark I would leave on this planet. I redefined myself over and over until I was crystal clear about who I was and then directed all that straight at the business.

Were all those business trainings and years of advice in vain? Not at all. Upon discovering who I was, I had a crystal clear idea of what tools were needed to reach my goals. Things were different this time around. My confidence was restored and I felt like I was making a difference. A very different type of customer started coming to my door.

I began to sell in a very different manner. A new version of my company that was fulfilling and profitable emerged; one that fueled my passion for creativity and served my customers like never before.

I have 19 years of running my own business and reside in the world of small business from front to back every day. I'm an eager student of life and learning. As long as I have the desire to grow my business, I will face challenges. With all of this I believe, with complete conviction, that you will never hit your stride until you let go of the notion that your business solutions are outside of you or that you must abandon your dreams to fit into the marketplace mold. Your competitor does not dictate your growth, you do. By the end of this journey you will discover, like I did, that you hold the keys to success within you.

Now it's your turn! Conventional wisdom says you must look outward for answers from experts, but it's time to look within, to find that Zen within you and seek its counsel. This book will help you grow your business in a way that embodies you, affords prosperity, brings the right people into your life and serves a community of people who desire your products and services. It will take you to the Zen Side of Business Ownership.

So what will you find when you are there? What will your Zen Business Ownership look like? Will it be a company that generates profits while you contemplate the universe in a rock garden sipping Japanese green tea in a bamboo cup? It might be, but whatever you imagine, you have the power within to create it. How's that for a Zen future? You were drawn to this book now it's up to you to use it. Let's go.

INTRODUCTION
EVERYTHING BEGINS WITH YOU

An exciting adventure awaits; or rather a calming, meditative, Zen-like experience filled with explosive excitement. You are on the brink of unleashing the potential within you and your business. This book addresses the mindset needed to reach the Zen Side of Business Ownership featuring your mindset, not mine, not your family's, not the "experts" and especially not your competition's. The more honest you are with yourself about yourself - your preferences, your experiences, and your dreams - the more you will get out of this book. Don't be afraid to admit truths and desires that you have hidden away or simply abandoned. For many of us, the world has taught us to ignore characteristics within ourselves that bring us joy but to others might seem silly or irrelevant. Toss aside any inhibiting thoughts from family, friends, or other influential groups. Listen closely to the voice within and let this book unleash the great power that you hold in your being. There is no one path to the Zen Side of Business Ownership, but there is only one mindset that will lead you there. I will provide you with the metaphorical tray and the magnifying glass, but it is up to you to do the searching and sifting.

Consider this book a toolset packed with what you'll come to know as Your Zen Movements. Each is a totem that is yours to keep and call upon at a given moment in your business career. These powerful movements will become part of your life, absorbed into your inner emotional compass and merged with business practices that hoist you into a position of power. Whether it's the formidable Zen Pillar of Focus (Chapter 4), the full offense of Zen Pounce (Chapter 5), or your influential Zen Reflection (Chapter 3) these tools will stay with you long after you've turned the final page.

Throughout the book I never miss the opportunity to use an analogy. Analogies put a creative spin on the seemingly mundane comparative concepts found in business. For example, no one would ever expect to compare the idea of searching for the right customers to searching for a gold sock in a warehouse full of green ones. But in Chapter 7, I make full use of such a juxtaposition. Keep an open mind as we explore several hypothetical stories and colorful analogies to drive in key points.

This is not another "Market Your Way to Success Overnight" or "Slash Your Competitor Into Pieces" approach. Adhering to the principles outlined in this book will elucidate and stress the importance of being strategic and help you transcend the lifestyles and marketing ideologies of our time. It addresses the personal element of your business and its interaction with the world. This is also not just a "do this", "do that" guideline. There is nothing Zen about performing a task unless you understand its deeper impact. We are complex beings with the need to experience, to understand, to be understood, to create, to connect with others and to contribute to this world.

I offer proven strategies and practices and introduce these ideas through a new filter. Seeing the business world in a different light may take some adjustment, but it will make you come alive and resonate with your deeper emotional core. It's about knowing yourself from within and letting this understanding lead you on the path to making the right choices for your own growth and the growth of your business. What works for one business may not work for another. We are individuals. Our businesses are expressions of us. Why shouldn't we take the time to truly understand how to grow our businesses in a way that cultivates the very qualities of our own character?

This is best read in progression. Each chapter builds on the next with "aha" moments unfolding along the way. However, if you read a section out of turn, you won't ruin the flow. After all, what's wrong with a little outside-the-box thinking? By following the lessons and teachings outlined in these chapters and completing the exercises, you'll soon find yourself on the holistic Zen Side of

Business Ownership inside and out, truly serving this world as well as fulfilling your own passions.

Throughout these pages, you will encounter a total of 13 Zen Movements, a few of which I mentioned above. You may find a whole chapter devoted to one movement, others have been compiled together in a single chapter. All are equal in their importance as you travel toward the Zen Side of Business Ownership. With each Zen Movement comes a series of questions or drills. These exercises, which will take some time and thought to complete, are only as good as the effort you put forth. Go slow to get the most out of each of them.

Additionally, at the end of every chapter, you'll find a section entitled "Take Aways" which, through the use of bullet points, highlights the main points of the chapter. To maximize the effectiveness of this book, carefully consider these points and ensure that you have given them your full attention before you move onto the next chapter.

So, congratulations on getting this book into your hands or into your ears. I hope you are as excited as I was the moment I was inspired to write it. I wrote this book, not for myself, but for you, to share what I learned once I moved to the Zen Side of Business Ownership. My goal is to inspire and empower you to be the absolute truest version of yourself. Now, it's action time. This is your chance to create an experience that will change not only your business, but also the world. So let's start this educational journey together, turn the page and follow the path toward Zen!

BE A PART OF THE WHOLE

THE MARKETPLACE HAS BEEN WAITING FOR YOU.

I magine, for a moment, a contrasting world, one devoid of its most inspiring creatures in their element. A place where nature's unique creations turn away from their higher calling only to emulate an animal, insect, or a plant they are not; a discordant landscape where the butterfly passes on its transformative role to remain like the worm. One where the honeybee surrenders its daytime pollination to fly at night as a moth. An entire world where families of insects, plants, and animals never serve their true calling and therefore cease to be of service to the larger community in need. A world such as this would surely produce a series of catastrophic reversals affecting the delicate animal kingdom as we know it.

Now, imagine a marketplace comparatively compromised, one devoid of the rich character and unique innovation of each of its contributors. One affording only a generic mold, leaving buyers and consumers without the products and services they deserve; a world where businesses abandon their unique expression and instead strive to simply be a better copy of their competition. Without the unique contributions we as business owners infuse, the marketplace will become a lifeless, discordant platform unable to serve the greater community. A marketplace of businesses solely focused on grabbing market share instead of striving to be the best. Is this a future worth creating? I hope not. This planet was, designed with a diverse and uniquely flourishing strategy and we humans who inhabit it are, in fact, no different than our nature's counterparts. Inherent within all of Earth's beautiful creations is the desire to be truly unique. What a shame it would be to abandon your own business expression to be like another.

This book was created to help align you for great achievements utilizing your uniqueness as the cornerstone. Look past the idea of uniformity and dilution as long-term growth strategies and acknowledge your singular quirky perspective as the key to fulfillment and success. This is the moment to celebrate your idiosyncrasies and let them guide you in your creative decision making. Embrace those quirky mannerisms you're afraid to show the world. These are the very traits that make you special.

In the preface I defined where you needed to be to operate from the Zen Side of Business Ownership. Let's review it once again as this is the very foundation of what is to come in the following pages. Zen Business Ownership is…

An enterprise that:
1) truly embodies you
2) is profitable
3) creates a following of supporters
4) serves a community

This first chapter is your wake-up call. You are different, special, and perfectly unique. There is only one of you and there will only ever be one of you. It is your responsibility to make your uniqueness prominent in your business; to do everything in your power to separate yourself from others in the marketplace. It's time to consider your perspective, the very way you do things. Until now you might have been looking outward and seeing your uniqueness as a disadvantage, a limitation; the thing that's holding you back.

This misunderstanding couldn't be farther from the truth. In fact the exact opposite is true. There is an entire community of people out there who are waiting for something different. There is a group of buyers eager to see your industry change and serve them better. We live in a marketplace caught within the power struggle of a one-size-fits-all mentality and a rich, diverse, and endless world of options contrasting it. The single advantage you have in this world is your uniqueness. It is what will make you successful.

At this point, I want you to consider and remember this formula. You will be referring to it as you work your way through this book.

(A) Your unique qualities + (B) Your celebration and utilization of them = (C) success in the marketplace.

Celebrating your distinctive qualities means you will innately solve problems differently than your competitors. It will bring that spark back into business ownership, making the marketplace exciting once again. Not only for you as a business owner, but also for your consumers. Embracing your diversity is the game changer. By putting your unique perspective on business out there, you will attract the type of customer that wants more of what you have, not more of the same.

Do you have dreams about being as big as a Fortune 500 company? Then you'd better start thinking about how to solve the problems in your marketplace differently than your competition. You and all your eccentric qualities are your ticket to move the needle of experience, innovation, and advancement. Make your mark and service the world of commerce in a way no-one else can. Perhaps for the first time in your career, truly serve a community of people and fulfill your new Zen Element #4.

MOVEMENT 1: YOUR ZENERSITY

To get you headed on the path toward the Zen Side of Business Ownership, you must first discover your first Zen Movement - Your Zenersity.

A quick glance at our plant kingdom exemplifies the futility of a one-size-fits-all mentality. A young sprouting plant doesn't require the same amount of water as an adult tree. Too much water and it will die. Yet in business, there's a push to adopt every practice that has mainstream appeal. Why is this? It's true, all plants need basics; water, sun, air, soil. But as you move up the list of requirements, things become a bit more complicated. Some plants rely on region, altitude, or seasonal fires to thrive. Others utilize beauty, scent, or color to keep their species alive.

Is the natural world suggesting that you ignore dated methodologies and turn to modern trends for success? Should you abandon systems you know well in order to compete against a sprouting company? There are essentials within business; generally accepted foundations such as marketing, budgeting, goal setting, streamlining, etc. But there are an unlimited number of ways to address these points. Every business is different. In the plant kingdom, every species needs hydration of some sort, but not the same amount or delivered in the same way. You can't use a seasonal forest fire approach to make a rose garden thrive. Still, many of us find ourselves adopting the latest trends and wondering why we aren't getting the same results as the innovators of them. Exploring trends, experimenting, and adopting new methods are mandatory in the name of growth. You should utilize the tools that speak to you. What is so cutting edge about copying the business next door? The real challenges for success are not between you and a competitor. It's between you and your business. Diversity is what the marketplace has been waiting for and where the Zen Side of Business Ownership begins to take shape.

Overcoming these everyday challenges in a manner that is unique to you is the making of your competitive advantage for long-term growth. Look closely at what's exciting for you and how it embodies your character, and leverage that information. Like all nature's creatures, you may innately know the strategies that work for you. Look deeper within to find your personal recipe for success. You can only achieve these discoveries by starting with a metaphorical clean sheet of paper to brainstorm and intuit what solutions will best serve you. There's already a distinctly unique competitive advantage within you and it won't take much digging to start a proverbial downpour of ways to unleash it. Celebrating them proudly is your ticket to hyperspace business growth. Welcome to your first Zen Movement - Your Zenersity! This is what you get when you combine Zen with Diversity. Call it a merging of sorts. Call it zany. Call it quirky. Call it whatever you want. But, never under any circumstances, call it "ordinary." Because Your Zenersity is an expression of you.

I define Zenersity as follows:

Zenersity - *noun /zə'nərsədē/ - personal distinct, one-of-a-kind qualities, fitted harmoniously to you. (Otherwise known as your new trusted advisor.)*

From here on, turn to Your Zenersity to find tailored solutions for the challenges set before you; solutions truly custom-fitted to every nook and cranny of the business you are rearing. Are you working on marketing copy that could use a certain flair? Consult Your Zenersity. Trying to scale production in a way that suits your unique space and workforce? Turn to Your Zenersity. Does your coffee business have roasting challenges unique to you? Zenersity time.

You've likely spent most of your career forcing yourself to adopt practices not natural to you. Those days are numbered as you can now turn to your trusted Zenersity. Learn to embrace it. Own it. Be it. For it is all of your quirky mannerisms in a single word. Your preferences. Your distinct qualities. Your competitive edge. It is your unique vantage point on the world and the key to your fulfillment for successes to come. Understanding and incorporating Your Zenersity is the one single biggest action you can take to progress your business and finally serve a community in a way no one else can. The journey ahead will ensure you get every opportunity to sharpen and integrate Your Zenersity. It starts now - Exercise #1 is here.

Define Your Zenersity

You have a distinctly unique competitive advantage within you waiting to be unleashed, and now it's time to let it out. Welcome to your first assignment. Below is a list of categories to populate. Write down the personality traits that define you - these are jewels of information to discover Your Zenersity.

Before you get started, here are a few things to consider as you work through this first exercise. Take the time you need to think about your answers. Try to list at least three answers for each question. Grab a partner if it helps get the creative process going. But it is imperative that the answers come from you. Answer with complete conviction, knowing full well you can stand behind every quality as your own, not what someone else thinks about you. Regardless of any inhibitions, dive in! What qualities about you get your heart racing? What are the skillsets you possess that make you feel alive? What problem-solving characteristics do you have that no one else does? This entire program, beginning with this first exercise, is dependent on how you put yourself on paper. Find the time to address this step correctly. Look within, be honest with yourself, and begin to put it in writing.

Exercise 1A

1. **1. Ideologies:** What viewpoints or ways of performing activities are unique to you?
2. **Proficiencies:** What qualities demonstrate your aptitudes and ability to accomplish the things you set out to do?
3. **Ethics:** What are your qualities that demonstrate trustworthiness? What shows your ability to keep a promise?

4. **Influences:** Who or what things are most influential to your character?
5. **Outward Eccentricities (Style):** What are the personal touches or ways of outwardly expressing yourself that define you?

6. **Service Characteristics:** How do you show the world or those around you that you care?

Congratulations on taking the first step into what will now become your new modus operandi: writing down all of the qualities that make you, you. However intricate, seemingly ineffective, or silly these qualities may seem, start assembling them into your playbook to use for every challenge you may encounter from here on. If you've struggled in any way, not to worry, there will be plenty of time to finesse your answers in future chapters. There is more "unique" to celebrate. Imagine a world where choices and rich diversity abounds and all would finally strive to be their very best! This Zen future is attainable. It's just a quirky personality away!

You have just created Your Zenersity. Take note of it. Begin to foster it. Make it the centerpiece of your business decision making and hold on for dear life as the world around you transforms in a way you could never have imagined. That wasn't so hard and now you can see the results. For when you divide yourself into these six categories and multiply each by three unique traits, you get nothing short of a big gorgeous pile of Your Zenersity. Onward to the next Zen Movement.

MOVEMENT 2: YOUR ZEN OFFERING

Water - one of the most beautiful elements of this planet – is perhaps the greatest example of Zen. It encompasses much of Earth's surface, expanding far beyond the spherical curvature, weaving its way as it performs its symbiotic duties. Whether in gaseous form, liquid, solid, or infinite combinations of these, this compound pervades as far as the eye can see. Wherever you explore, water is there. Water is beautiful, nourishing, and life-giving. Its exchange and contribution affords continued existence everywhere. Every organism depends upon its availability and exchange.

There is a parallel to be drawn between the compound of water and your business, because your own creation is just as beautiful and magical as nature's counterpart. It contains a similarly infinite array of diverse facets and inter-workings harmoniously operating in varying capacities to help the greater community you are drawn to serve. Every moment creating an unending combination of deliverables to the world. But does this mean your future growth plan is an endless list of infinities, intricacies, and complexities? It would be quite an undertaking to calculate all the configurations for delivering a given service, right? That expansive proposition hardly embodies the word Zen.

It would be hard to argue that your business could be

best described as an exchange of goods, a sort of this for that. No matter how you spin it, you offer something for something, a product or service in exchange for currency. But is this the picture of a Zen offering you aspire to achieve? Ask yourself this basic, but vitally important question. What element(s) are you exchanging and to what end? You might feel compelled to state the obvious; you're exchanging this widget or service for a profit. Be careful. In answering so, you still have one foot pointed down un-Zen alley. True, your widget is integral to the business equation; but this book isn't about simply handing over a widget. Per the Zen Side of Business Ownership you have to include something "more" in the very thing that you offer the world.

Look closely at our aqueous counterpart for a moment. Viewing water from a scientific lens, one would see that despite the infinite variety of its expression, it is surprisingly basic at its core, two elements, hydrogen and oxygen (H_2O) working in tandem. It is nothing short of miraculous that the whole of its behavior and assistance on this earth can be born from such an elemental simplicity. Well, at your business's most basic level, it can be expressed as a succinct formula much the same. The totality of your business and the experiences of those who interact with it can be broken into a similar fundamental.

Observe a business at its most basic level, and you will find a gap in the "generally accepted" offering equation. An elusive component that if excluded, will be detrimental to the overall successes you are striving to achieve.

Although it could be easy to miss this delta, not including it will inhibit future growth and the opportunities to scale it as powerfully and as naturally as our fluid example. Can you guess what that element might be? Here's a hint. It starts with the letter "Z."

Circle back to the question, what are you exchanging? Take your capacity (C) - your ability to create, manufacture or provide a product or service. Then, raise that to the power of Zenersity $(^Z)$ - your personal distinct, one of a kind qualities. You are exchanging a widget raised to the power of Zenersity - specifically, yours. $C^Z = YZO$ - the perfect blend of your company's ingredients, factored by you, into something as capable, intricate and amazing as any one of nature's creations. Your Zen Offering (YZO). Voila. You're no longer just exchanging a widget. How's that for Zen science at work!

Let's put Your Zen Offering to the test. The sandwich shop next to you has the same floor plan and buys from the same food supplier. They have the same (C). What can you deduce about your competitive predicament here? Are you now bound to offer a better version of the menu options they have or simply lower prices? Many business owners find themselves looking at their growth strategies from this generally accepted lens. Constantly employing the "one up" strategy to advance their business predicament. Well, it's time for a new lens. Apply the Zen formula $(C^Z = YZO)$ and you'll get a more definitive answer and the ability to enter the marketplace with the perfect marriage of your resources to the power of Your

Zenersity, making an exchange that will serve the community of patrons in a way that no one else can touch. If Your Zen Offering is a product or service that only you can deliver, you have a winning strategy for the growth. The concept of scaling from a core competency is the heart and soul of a business poised for great contributions to this world. You already have the craft, but from here forward, you can't have a business unless there's a Zen Offering to see it through. It has very little to do with the product you are making and much more to do with how you leverage Your Zenersity. So is it time to start planning the same menu options as the sandwich joint next door? The Zen answer is no. ($C^Z = YZO$) is your new business model.

How will Your Zenersity make any difference? You put sesame seeds on your bread and the place next door uses pepper. A sandwich is still a sandwich, right? Hardly. Admire our fluid companion more closely. Water would express a completely different narrative for each of its manifestations. For the animal world, Water is vegetation. For communities of people Water is farming and irrigation. For our safari friends, water is a solitary oasis. And for the artist, water is a puddle reflecting the sky. The expression of water in all of its forms is utter perfection. It is time to reinvent your craft and its delivery. Push past the idea that your business has anything to do with the guy next to you because it has everything to do with how you package and deliver it via Your Zenersity. Only you hold the recipe. You have the power to rediscover the exchange between you and your customer. What would your sandwich business look like with the Zen Formula? For a child, a sandwich could be an afternoon out after school. For a couple, a sandwich could be a time to connect. For a team, a sandwich could be a way to celebrate a victory. For a philanthropist, a sandwich could be a way to feed the hungry.

Your Zen Offering can match each of these needs. With Your Zenersity you can create a menu set and environment to refresh the customer forging lasting experiences and deeper connections with your patrons. Your Zen Offering is the catalyst, directly responsible for the community of people you serve, to connect and experience life in a new way that only you can facilitate. It aligns your business into a series of actions that resonates with your character. How is that for a Zentastic proposition?

Exercise 1B

Revisiting the question about the element(s) you are exchanging and to what end, try this experiment using a new formula to create your own Zen Offering. Whose offering is this? Your Zen Offering. Not your neighbor's. Not your competition's. This is your chance to proclaim to the world who you are. You have a business and therefore you have the capacity to change how business is done.

Before you complete the exercise below, let me provide a few examples. Say you run an *accounting business (C)* and have a *creative passion and aptitude for the dance (Z)*. Perhaps you were an artist yourself? Imagine being the best financial advisor and tax expert available to individuals and small businesses as they seek to establish a stable financial base in the unpredictable world of the arts. That's Your Zen Offering:

Creating a solid financial footing for performers who work with you (YZO).

Or maybe you run a *machining company (C)* and *love world travel and enjoy rich culture (Z)*. What better way to add value to your customers than to be:

The company that researches and incorporates manufacturing methods from around the world (YZO).

Imagine the advantage you would have with offerings such as these?

So it's time to uncover Your Zen Offering (C^Z = YZO). Fill in the blanks on the following statement:

I will be the first in my industry to combine _____ (C)_____ raised to new levels of _____ (Z)_____ and/to create _____ (YZO)_____ for my customers.

How do you know if you've hit the nail on the head with Your Zen Offering? Once you find it, you will know plain and simple. You'll light up and see all your beautiful Zenergistic qualities beginning to circle around causing an uncanny spring in your step. If not take a second and perfect it. Stay with it! Finesse it! Refine it! It will pay dividends. It's time to embrace, embody, and focus your unique character within your business and set forth in motion milestones you never thought possible. You'll be a trend setter, not a trend follower. You can accomplish great things for this world when you let Your Zenersity be your guiding light and create Your Zen Offering born from your truest character.

Chapter Take Aways

To get to the Zen Side of Business Ownership, you must incorporate all four of these fundamental elements in all aspects of your business as the Zen Side of Business Ownership is defined as:

An enterprise that:

1. truly embodies you
2. is profitable
3. creates a following of supporters
4. serves a community

Your Zenersity, your tool to establish your special niche and your business's value added, is derived from six categories to which you assign three traits unique to you. These categories are:

1. Ideologies (Personal Philosophies)
2. Your Proficiencies

3. Your Ethics
4. Your Influences (Muse, Inspirations)
5. Your Eccentricities (Style)
6. Your Service Characteristics

Your Zen Offering, which can translate into a tradition mission statement, establishes your creative spin, creates a sustainable value proposition and translates passion within your business. Use this formula to hone in on your true Zen Offering:

I will be the first in my industry to combine _____ (C)_____ raised to new levels of _____ (Z)_____ and/to create _____ (YZO)_____ for my customers.

2

FIND YOUR ESSENCE

YOU STAND FOR SOMETHING. DISCOVER IT!

Anchors aweigh. Bon voyage. You've set your course, dialed in your offerings from Chapter One and now it is time to set sail. It's you and the proverbial ocean of opportunity. You've found yourself, discovered what you have to offer this world. You and your business are what the ocean of commerce has been missing. With a newfound confidence in all you have to offer, you are set to fill that missing link perfectly. There's a purpose worth pursuing and people will now benefit from Your Zenersity. Take a moment and pat yourself on the back. You are on the path to fulfillment.

But don't break that bottle of champagne against the bow just yet. There's more to the Zen equation. You are moving forward with an offering that may be different than the one you initially started. Your sails are rigged to a new course and heading into uncharted waters. So, while having a clear idea of the linchpin to Zen business success, simply dialing in Your Zen Offering alone won't ensure that you hit your new target. You now need new tools to navigate. You're at the helm, in the captain's chair, making the calls, but be wary as the formidable world of commerce can make the art of growing a business venture more complex than it needs to be, creating a seemingly endless path of twist and turns.

You have a destination and a seaworthy vessel but the real work starts now. Unfortunately the path to the Zen Side of Business Ownership is not necessarily lined with the calming reverent seas. There will be plenty of waves and currents to throw you off course; an ever-mounting stream of circumstances requiring the highest levels of stability to endeavor. Whether you're a one-man show or have staff aboard, there's only one person you can turn to to get your organization to safe harbor. You are the navigator who directs your course to success. This is your business and only you have the passion, knowledge and creative force to direct you to your target efficiently. Defining yourself and what you stand for allows you to clearly see potential obstacles and opportunities. For without a powerful compass to chart your course and gauge your progress, how can you tackle stormy conditions? As you steer into the daunting seas that await, how will you know which waves your vessel can endure and which ones will thrash you back to shore?

Not to worry. This chapter will equip you with a navigation system like no other. A set of parameters for you, determined by you, to set the very stage for what undertakings are worth pursuing and which ones will toss you about like a ship lost at sea. The time has come to own the captain's chair and declare what you stand for; what your business stands for. You will establish your personal manifesto. Your new *modus operandi*! The **Highest Probability Tool (HPT)** that will serve as the best path between where you are now and the manifestations of your newfound offering.

Defining your essence is the magical compass that will assess the terrain ahead and factor your ship's capability to navigate it. Like a stream of water flowing down a pronounced terrain, you will weave about the topography, finding the most harmonious path to your final destination. It is time to establish the clear boundaries for what potential entanglements are worthy of facing straight on and which unforeseen disturbances are detrimental and to be avoided.

This is more than simply establishing a set of core values. It is adopting a sophisticated navigation system that will cut through the densest fog and warn you to veer from alluring shallow reefs. It is a piercing beam of light to keep you from following paths that are not in alignment with your goals and which will finally stack the deck in your favor. If you have the proper navigation tools and stay the steady course, you will be in a position of great power; one that will put you on the fast track to predictable growth. It is time to own your essence by standing firmly at the command console and experiencing the Zen Side of Business Ownership as you create an organization that truly embodies you - Zen Element #1.

You are about to discover and master the very strategies that will ensure that the decisions you make and the agreements you establish are the right ones - poised for success. It's not as easy as saying yes to every sale that comes your way. You must have calculated actions planned as you survey a vast ocean of potential customers. You are the self-appointed one to navigate the very path that will lead Your Zen Offering smoothly through the seas ahead. The notion that running a business guided from your inner passion and character is the key to success is the purpose of this book.

This position of power carries with it a corresponding responsibility, one of keen insight into self, a deep knowing of who you are through and through. From head to toe, top to bottom, you must be completely aware of your strengths, innate talents, preferences and offerings if you're to move through this journey with gusto and hit your target. You will be challenged from virtually every direction imaginable. You must declare what you stand for and what you don't.

Like the plant analogy in Chapter One, you cannot deliver that which you are not equipped to deliver. Try as hard as you like, but it's impossible to persuade an apple tree to sprout oranges. The same goes for you. Your strengths inherently come with a corresponding capacity, a range of services you can deliver before you are extended beyond your capability. Simply understanding your idiosyncrasies serves a greater portion of your effectiveness in business. But it takes another level of commitment to create your own manifesto. You don't just have to know who you are, you have to live who you are. If you've created a business that resonates with the core of your being, then this is where your next Zen Movement will pay dividends. Put on your "Sunday best" and prepare to meet yourself, perhaps for the first time.

MOVEMENT 3: YOUR ZEN CODE
Temet Nosce
"Know Thyself" (Know Thy Business!!!)

At some time, most of us consider the question – "Who am I and why am I here? Greek philosophers set the world in motion with these profound thoughts that transcend time. They knew a thing or two about the Zen Side of Business Ownership and unknowingly laid the groundwork for what this chapter addresses - the ability to examine one's life to its fullest and to put those strengths to work in life and in business. How does one begin to chart the course to the island of Zen Business Ownership? Hop back into the captain's chair and let's begin to navigate through Your Zen Code.

A seasoned captain knows every square inch of his or her vessel and to what extent it can be stressed, all the details integral to the survival on the seas. Your ability to weather the stormy seas ahead depends on getting to truly know yourself and your business for the first time. This will require asking questions that may not have occurred to you before. There's so much ahead to uncover about your business, about you and it is imperative that you understand the detriment of veering from your path. For every formidable wave heading toward you, you have the choice to power through it or turn towards a break on either side. There could be something that draws you in with its safe appeal, perhaps one lined with short term financial benefit. Be careful, here is where your voyage may start to veer.

Say your business finds and delivers the best possible apple to your clients, but the competition is making a killing selling oranges. What do you do? There's a fine line between working within the strengths of your essence and adapting to market changes to grow your business. There will be times when the business next to you is making a killing selling widgets that don't interest you. Do you follow their lead? Not if Your Zen Code dictates otherwise. But how can you know?

There will be plenty of conditions to negotiate along the way including popular trends, industry breakthroughs or advancements from your perceived competitors. You need to stay focused and run your own race. Always keep a weather eye out for happenings in your marketplace but as a veteran captain you'll need to distinguish the good currents from the bad. Not all distractions are detrimental. There will be great opportunities as well. Keep a firm grasp of what opportunities and customer promises are good for your company and how it pairs with Your Zen

Offering. You will be pulled in multiple directions and will have to deal with these encounters in one way or another. Are your customers asking you for deals and lower pricing to make the sale? Alluring currents come in all shapes and sizes. Should you make adjustments for each of your customers to keep their business? Risk every part of your niche and efficiencies to capture alluring fish swimming by? Or possibly worse, are you staying in calm waters never moving forward?

We, as the constant pleasers we tend to be, spend much of our time making sure that we leave a wake of happy customers. We can find ourselves continuously caught in the throes of where our inner passions guide us and where stresses point. Your passion to explore opportunities are often contrasted by a safe familiarity to set anchor. Facing the unknown and trudging forward into the dark abyss can be daunting.

It's time to "know thyself" and see things for what they are. To navigate on your true path. This is the chapter where your inner searching can truly shape the efforts of your business. This is the moment where you take your stance, know your essence, and own your spot in the marketplace with full force. You love and deliver apples like nobody else. So why sell oranges?

Are you looking for the auto-pilot button on your vessel or are you ready to establish who you are and draw a line in the sand? The questions that follow will make very clear how you will move onward and at what speed. It's time to turn on the **"HPT"** navigation system and with that flick of a switch comes reflection. These questions are designed to stop you in your tracks. Do not speed through and take a break if you get overwhelmed. For these six questions will force you to carefully search within for your new road map and set of actions that will turn your business into a focused effort. They will push you to see a new more powerful version of your enterprise.

The Zen Side of Business Ownership is where you are headed. In the last chapter you found your Zenersity, creating a stable foundation for this drill. What is the Zen Code this book is now advocating? Like all of the Zen Movements outlined on the following pages, this is a concept so simple at its core that it contains the universal power to yield something much grander.

To discover Your Zen Code, you'll need to revisit the questions from Chapter One as needed. There's an immediate benefit to analyzing yourself on paper and being brutally honest with yourself is the only way to truly come to the answers that can change your business. Only you have the wherewithal to create your manifesto. It may not happen overnight, but stay the course. Dive deep and watch the tide turn in your favor.

Exercise 2A

I've provided examples and analogies to help you truly understand the purpose of each exercise and question. These exercises take time and thoughtfulness. The effort you put into each will help define you and your business.

This chapter is about discovering Your Zen Code. To do so, you'll be developing a set of six axioms that make up that code. These exercises and questions will help you construct Your Zen Code and move you toward the Zen Side of Business Ownership.

1) What is the philosophy or "take" for which you want to be known?

What is the single most important outcome born from Your Zen Offering; the quality that will be obvious when a customer evaluates your services? This is the paradigm shift you stand for - the thing you do differently than the business next to you.

Need some clarity? Here is an example. You are a teacher of young children and your bottom line is to instill a love of learning for every child. When a potential parent meets with you, the first thing you might say is "I create a "love of learning" and my aim is to ensure your child will have a passion for education and self-directed study for the entirety of his or her life." Wow! Can you imagine working with such a teacher?

Or maybe you are an interior decorator with a passion for efficiency. Saving young families from the stresses of the disorganization that inherently comes with growth? Your ultimate goal is to remove stress and clutter from their lives by creating intuitive storage spaces and layouts. How might you greet your potential customers? "Every one of my efforts is directed towards organization and saving you time so that you can focus on the things that matter – an organized and happy family".

There's no right or wrong to what you decide, but you must defend it at all costs. Our teacher above may be tempted to offer preparatory test taking strategies that are not in alignment with his or her philosophy because the competition is doing it, but should steer clear of the alluring current and continue full speed ahead toward defined goals.

There's a fine line between adding value to your organization with more tools and veering off course thereby diluting your offering. The answer to this question will be the quality you stand for from here forward. Whatever it is, stay the course. Veering from any one of Your Zen Code attributes may spell the beginning of a lost at sea adventure. There is so much in store that will be yours for the taking if you stand firm in your philosophy.

As you answer the question above, refer to your answers from Chapter One, Exercise 1A , #1, to help you define your philosophy.

2) Considering your answer to question #1 above, how will you define your product?

What are you selling? What is the actual service offered? What are you delivering? Consider this the guarantee you hold in front of your customer and say, "This is what you're getting." Simply handing over a widget, however, is not what this book is about. There's more. Specifically, what aspect of Your Zen Offering is contained within it? Your finished product is for you to create. This is the new metrics by which you will now be measured. You must deliver it every time; not just once, not to every other customer, all of the time.

Decide what you are delivering. Dream big. This new standard by which you and your staff operate is a way to measure your efforts and gauge your progress. The teacher in the previous example promises students who actively engage in learning without coercion or incentives. How could someone say no to a value added such as that? So, what is your finished product? The possibilities are as expansive as the seas you are navigating. It's exciting to think about all the ways you can package up that unique thing you offer from an all-inclusive perspective. Points are awarded for creativity. Take your tangible item and philosophy and what do you get? You are on the right track when you light up and realize that no competitor can even come close to what you offer. It's time to get thinking. Let's have it.

Referring to your answers from Chapter One, Exercise 1A, #2, will help you define your product offering.

3) What singular promise will you make to ensure the delivery of your product from question #2?

You must be willing, at all costs, to deliver your newly defined product. It's not enough to promise. Your efforts must be fully supported and foolproof. What specific things are you willing to do in order to hit the target? Mistakes can and will happen. Emergencies will arise. Weather conditions change. But you must make good on delivery. You have to be committed in all respects, which means hedging your resources to ensure you'll never have to say "I'm so sorry it is just not ready."

Good intentions are a great sentiment, but a solid promise to focus your resources towards success is even better. You will be light years ahead of your competition in the customer satisfaction department. Are they making a solemn promise to their customers or are they making excuses? It really doesn't matter because you are running your own race with your own solid promise. What's it going to be? Jot it down.

Use to the qualities listed from Chapter One, Exercise 1A, #3, as you determine your promise to deliver.

4) What resources will you consult when problem solving to uphold your singular promise from question #3 above?

Customers are the final judges of whether or not you upheld your side of the deal. That's just the reality, so best get used to it. You can usually gauge the success of your efforts in the form of a smile and their return business. It's your responsibility to do everything possible to uphold your commitments. But, sometimes, even with all the preparations you've made, things get crazy. When life throws you that proverbial curve ball you must be ready.

Who or what will you turn to when things don't go according to plan? You need a trusted, consistent source of material for problem-solving and strategic maneuvering to weather the tides ahead.

More importantly, if you have a staff, they need every resource possible to make decisions that ultimately act in the best interest of your company, uphold your integrity, and make sure your product gets delivered as promised. By default, most problems will land at your feet, but there is only so much of you to go around. Who or what will you consult? Be specific. Are there works of art, literature, cultural or other philosophical axioms that you reference as your guiding light? What existing business practices speak to you?

Obstacles and challenges are a part of life. A guiding light to reference can ease your worries. So what is it? What is your playbook of inspiration? How you handle adversity is often the make or break for customer loyalty. With your trusted playbook, you will be fully prepared to operate when things don't go your way. When your customer needs your product or services again, they will remember the time you kept it together when the going got tough.

So, what's it going to be? What will you lean on to firmly plant your feet in the marketplace as a force you know yourself to be?

Look to your list from Chapter One, Exercise 1A, #4, it will help guide you to build your playbook for success.

5) What is your signature flair?

How will you express yourself and your business? Your business can, and must have an attitude; one that screams Your Zen Offering. So much so that your customers can't help but notice. It's your "vibe," the "thing" by which people will remember you. This is your signature flair. Specifically, something that addresses the five senses. What will your customers see, hear, taste, touch, or smell to remember you and your business? Is it something you say to your clients after every sale? Is it a greeting, a special way that only you interact with them? What are the elements that convey your essence to your internal team as well as the outside customers so they can feel, experience, and get to know what you are about? This signature should be something that will imprint a mark on them forever.

Distinguishing traits are defined by your character and larger life experiences. Think of a favorite song, movie or cultural influence. What inspired you to start a business? What personal elements are integral to your character and thus, the larger enterprise of your business? More than likely the same things that bring you fulfillment will be that which you want to share with your customers moving forward.

Consider how will, and won't, your staff express themselves? What is your "signature"? What is your business's "signature?" It's time to write them down. Lay out the sounds, imagery, smells and tactile frequencies all customers will experience while interacting with you and your staff. Is it a minimalist themed interior space? Is it the gratuitous use of a striking color on your walls? It's time to put in writing the very portion of your identity that you hold as your own; to solidify your company's image in the marketplace. Define your offering. You get to decide.

Referring to the qualities listed in Chapter 1, Exercise 1A, #5, will help you create your signature flair.

6) How will you inspire the larger community?

How will you impact your community? How can you improve it or endow it with some aspect of Your Zen Offering for its betterment? Accessing the highest levels of your truest character means understanding your impact on a grander scale.

It's entirely up to you how you help save the world. This doesn't mean you have to adopt the philanthropic view of supporting all inhabitants on earth. Discover something that is achievable and feasible from your perspective and resources. Search your heart. Look diligently for solutions that are born directly from your immediate passions and resources before endowing the world your time or money.

Your community is craving a meaningful connection. A shining light of a business imbuing the world with a contribution that isn't only about what money can buy. For example, the owner of a dance studio could work to make dance more visible to the community. Something that inspires people to engage and support the arts and urges them to see the rich diversity and creativity that this world can hold. For our interior decorator mentioned above, it could be the very end product - happier more organized parents that go on to raise the attitudes of their kids and others around them. How's that for improving a corner of the earth?

Quality wins over quantity in the Zen world. By default, reaching the Zen Side of Business Ownership automatically has you as a shining inspiration for all those around you. Consider your relationship with yourself as the key to connecting with others. This is a "you being you challenge".

On what part of this planet will you shine the light of truth and inspiration to shift it for the better? You get to decide. Points are awarded for most effective and original. But don't worry. You can't lose when you mix two extremely powerful words - Zenersity and Inspiration. Just go for it.

Refer to your qualities from Chapter One, Exercise 1A , #6, to help create your community impact.

Your Zen Code Initialized

Clarity sequence, initiated. Success. You've done it. Take a deep breath. But don't adjust your sails just yet. You're one degree shy of your perfect course. It's time to initialize Your Zen Code.

You've taken the time and discovered what only few

have done for their business – defined direction and clarity. You've cracked the code on one of the hardest challenges you will face in your business career. You've earned your bars. Feel confident and ready to take the helm?

You are a force to be reckoned with in the marketplace, fueled by your passions. You have discovered your essence, yourself, and your direction in business and laid your path. When the dust clears from this exercise you will find yourself in a world of enlightenment, clarity, and opportunity. For these drills serve a grand purpose – they benefit you. If you stay the course, clearer waters are ahead. It's time to gather your answers and create a resource manual, your playbook. Your next stop, Port Di Manifesto!

Exercise 2B

Round up your answers from Exercise 2A above and place them in the corresponding lines below. Recite each line and copy it to your new playbook. Refer to it regularly, everyday if you need it.

Zen Code Axiom # 1

The reason for continually creating this business enterprise is *(Insert 2A.1)*.

Zen Code Axiom # 2

Every part of my being, organization, and staff is directed to *(Insert 2A.2)*.

Zen Code Axiom # 3

For every sale that travels through my enterprise, above all else, I will uphold the following commitment *(Insert 2A.3)*.

Zen Code Axiom # 4

In the interest of keeping my customer promise, I will always retreat to *(Insert 2A.4)* to be the guiding light for crossroad decisions.

Zen Code Axiom # 5

I will employ and ensure that my environment always embodies *(Insert 2A.5)* as a defining component and identity to which my company, staff, contractors, and other partners will universally uphold.

Zen Code Axiom # 6

My organization imbues the world with *(Insert 2A.6)*.

Your Zen Code Finalized

These six axioms represent Your Zen Code, by which your business will now operate. Your **HTP** system has been activated and is now online. Sit back and enjoy this revelation. In their simplest form, you've created six guiding light axioms born from the very categories of your Zenersity exercise. Axioms that establish the solid grounding of who you are and where you will operate, for these Axioms will make decisions very black and white. Congratulations for making it through this segment and through these difficult questions. If you haven't completed all of them to the extent you know you can, you can always reflect further. The entirety of this guide will help continue to focus your efforts until you are a powerful Zen machine.

Let's look at Your Zen Code more closely. All facets of you are now pointed the same direction. Every portion of your being is aligned and directed to one goal, one mission, one destination. Things are as clear as tropical waters. A potential drift off-course will show up on your radar instantly. You have no excuses for allowing actions that don't serve your business. There is no longer justification for weight that holds you back, no more falling for detrimental short-term currents.

You can now see what resources and opportunities are directly in alignment with Your Zen Offering and which ones are not. You know whether selling oranges is a golden opportunity or a perilous wave of dilution in disguise. You know which waves to ignore, which waves are worthy of trudging through and which ones to steer from hard. Your newly established Zen Code will ensure that anyone or anything that threatens the integrity of your offering gets thrown overboard.

Some hard decisions may be in order regarding habits that are unhealthy for your enterprise. It will be clear as day when things drift off course. Stand firm as the formidable captain and stop these actions swiftly. Take Your Zen Code out for a spin. Get to know it, inside and out. Tell your customers. Put a copy of it on the wall to see every day. Start analyzing your daily actions to see which ones are helping you grow towards it. Start looking at what tools and purchases support Your Zen Code and you will begin to realize the new efficiencies and opportunities you can confidently take on.

Feel like a tiny ship in the middle of a vast ocean? Hardly. You are ready to take the helm! There's an uncanny confidence about you. You now have direction, purpose. You can create an offering that no one else can. You ought to be beaming with energy and excitement charging forward on the seven seas ahead of you. Crack that bottle of champagne against the bow and celebrate your maiden voyage with Your Zen Code navigating. I wish you all the best with your journey. I know without a doubt it will be Zentastic!

Chapter Take Aways

Your Zen Code is comprised of six axioms that will guide you to the Zen Side of Business Ownership. This invaluable playbook or, simply put, your new set of core values, will be what you turn to as you create new performance metrics, define your customer promise, create a baseline for the culture of your business and begin successful growth.

Your Zen Code's Six Axioms

1. The reason for continually creating this business enterprise is *"x"*.
2. Every part of my being, organization, and staff is directed to *"x"*.
3. For every sale that travels through my enterprise, above all else, I will uphold the following commitment *"x"*.
4. In the interest of keeping my customer promise, I will always retreat to *"x"* to be the guiding light for crossroad decisions.
5. I will employ and ensure that my environment always embodies *"x"* as a defining component and identity to which my company, staff, contractors, and other partners will universally uphold.
6. My organization imbues the world with"x".

CREATE YOUR SPACE

SCALING YOUR HEAVEN ON EARTH MEANS PUTTING
"YOU" IN IT.

P utting a motivational poster on the wall is a good place to start on the journey of creating your space. But, believe it or not, it is not only the poster you choose, but also the process by which you hang it that will deliver the Zen you are seeking. Your approach to creating a space from the Zen Side of Business Ownership can make or break the stability of your business. There's so much more than meets the eye to this seemingly simple task of plastering your favorite inspirational image next to your desk. It needs to be absolutely perfect.

You may think there are far more important tasks to complete. Not true. Your company's future is on the line here and the energy you put forth into placing it "ever just so" determines the success of your company now and in future years. While many would pass at the opportunity to turn a poster hanging into a three-hour project, I'll give you the answer why you need to take your time. Whether you have already set up your space or you're just starting, this easy to overlook addressing of steps is the foundation in which all future expansion, methods, SOPs, staff collaboration, and organization will be built upon.

I'm not being overly dramatic when I stress that everything hinges on this one little task of hanging your poster. Every corner systematically laid down in the same order, one after the other. It matters. You need to do this by the book, by Your book. Taking your space and everything that happens within it seriously is the make or break for growth, that super growth you dream about. The kind of growth that will find you working in an environment that fosters efficiency, communication and camaraderie all resulting in success and prosperity for you, for your staff and your clients.

By the end of this chapter you won't let one corner or measurement go unnoticed. Attention to the smallest detail will put you on the track to ultimate scalability. Whether they are placed perfectly level or perfectly crooked or even upside-down is yours to implement. Whether you use tape, or tacks, or gum, you can not let one corner out of your sight.

Every poster, pen, tack, and notepad you pick up, lay down, place in your drawer, and put on your desk with the same deliberate movements, will be a glamorous victory that further extends the impact of your space for you and those who use it. Keep at it, and you will soon reach a state where your workspace is a perfect reflection of you in your truest light. While some might label this "company systems" in disguise, creating your space is so much more. It is the creation of a workspace that screams your essence, your mission, and your methods. It is a place that now directly guides the company, its employees, and even the clientele to perform in a manner that continuously aligns your business harmoniously with your offering. A working machine modeled by you and your methods that will draw the right people into the right actions. Or, better said, an organization that creates a following of supporters - Zen Element #3.

MOVEMENT 4: YOUR ZEN WAY

Take a look at your workspace for a moment and what takes place within it; all of that beautiful creativity and productivity. How do you currently undertake projects within the resources it affords? Don't you already do things in a manner that's unique to you?

I addressed the importance of celebrating your quirky uniqueness early in the book for a good reason. Because most of what you will be performing in your business will, by default, include the element of you. Would you currently try and put a poster on the wall in any other way than that which makes sense (to you)? You are very much unique in the way you perform your duties. Just ask your staff or your friends! If you try to divorce your actions from your style, what you're inevitably left with is a big pile of not you. It's time you leverage the skillset into something that will take your business to the next level and give it a name - Your Zen Way.

Think about the bigger picture at hand. Your unique way of doing things is great news. Because without putting your idiosyncratic methods front and center, you'll be selling your business short of the foundation it needs to grow; the thing that transforms your shining personality into productivity with lightning speed. Your Zen Way is the fastest, most direct route to super space scaling. Celebrating your unique qualities is the key to charging up your environment. It's time to include more of you in it; your ways, mannerisms, preferences, everything about you. With all this "you" around 24/7, it could begin to raise a few eyebrows. Ready to take your vanity out for a test spin?

Does celebrating your Zenersity mean killing the enthusiasm and camaraderie of your trusted team with too much focus on you? Hardly. The deeper you dive into Your Zen Way, the easier you will be making things for your staff, partners, suppliers and everyone involved in creating your offering. Instead of frustration, discouragement and do-overs, you'll have uncanny support brewing.

Let's use an example. You march yourself over to a local fast food business looking for employment. Burger-making anyone? You enthusiastically put on your apron and reach for a spatula. As you look around and sift through the drawers there's not a single item that even remotely resembles a utensil. You know your way around a kitchen, how to flip a patty and how to turn on a burner when everything is right there where you need it. But in this hi-tech industrial kitchen there is not even a grill. A hallway of massive stainless-steel monoliths with buttons and digital readouts surrounds you. This is frustrating! You've got a stack of frozen patties in one hand, and a slew of unhappy customers in the other.

Still think the poster hanging procedure is a waste of time? There's no way for you to possibly be able to step into this restaurant environment and be effective from the beginning. You have your way of cooking and the restaurant chain has theirs. Everyone has their own way of doing things.

Do you want your staff members to feel like you did in the aggravating example above? You absolutely cannot expect a new team member to come on board, follow your standard, and support Your Zen Way unless you've taken the time to establish it. So get comfortable with your idiosyncrasies quickly; understand and embrace your "style" of doing even the most menial of tasks and make it prominent throughout your business. This includes addressing our opening example. When a new team member comes on board, the first thing they must learn how to do is put a poster on the wall, your way. Every staff member will perform the task of poster-hanging in exactly the same way, every time.

Crazy talk? I don't think so. This concept is not news to our nation's top movers and shakers. They know this idea well and live it regularly. Established business leaders understand the value of systematic ways of working and the scalability it affords. Hopefully by this stage you've already taken ownership of your quirky mannerisms. So what's one more step? You simply need to document Your Zen Way. Teach it to all who interact with it. Write it down on a notepad, demonstrate it in a video, or diagram the steps with finger paint and plaster it on the wall. Make a sign. Anything. What is Your Zen Way to apply any poster that will possibly ever make its way onto a wall in your business?

Actual posters are not a determiner of success, it is symbolic. You don't need to hang a poster on the wall to create your following of supporters. You can hang nothing. You can paint, not paint, graffiti your space, polish or bulldoze the walls. Make an anti-space. Do it Your Zen Way.

You are the director and you've made a promise that your widget will be delivered just so. You must direct your staff in Your Zen Way. Then let them suggest more effective ideas that fit within your mold and your promise, per Your Zen Code. But be prepared, if there is one thing a business-owner should never say in front of staff members or partners, it is, "We really don't have a procedure for that."

You won't be that business owner because you have Your Zen Way and that way is the key. Your way is what generated the financial wherewithal to hire your staff in the first place. Your way is what differentiates you from the rest of the marketplace. Your way is the only thing you can count on for getting things done, your way. Establish your standard as a baseline now, revisions and growth can come later. Creating systems is something you do from the very beginning, even if you are a one man show. Don't wait. Start. Celebrate Your Zen Way. Savor it. Document it. Protect it. Trademark it. Reinforce it.

Basically, whatever you did to grow the company is what you need to continue to do. It's what your staff needs to continue to do. This growth wizardry means documentation. Just like the symbolic poster project you must have all Your Zen Ways laid out for complete duplication. So stop putting your Zenersity on the back shelf and start putting it down on paper, it's exercise time.

Exercise 3A.1

This exercise requires a notepad, chalkboard, a sheet of cardboard, or video camera, anything that stores information. You are going to discover Your Zen Way but first you need to do some research. Take a good look at yourself. Get a mirror if it helps. Take a photo of your facility. Note all of your idiosyncrasies - how you do things, especially mannerisms that stand out. How do you start your business day? Does it start with music? If so, what time? What station? What genre? Document it. Do you have team meetings? How many per week? Who leads them? How do they start? How do they end? Who participates? Document your routines. How do you take out the trash? Start at one side, end at another? How do you fold the bags? What color bags? How many do you order? Why? You don't use plastic? What then? Scrub your trashcans every week? With what scrubber? What color? How long are the bristles? Why? Document it all. The way you do things.

This is a personal logic exercise, not a pragmatist's approach. Start with easy things regardless of perceived importance. Basic functions. This may sound silly or feel like a waste of time, but trust me, you will see trends. A larger story will emerge from the small pieces and drills. More importantly, your staff will begin to pick up on these patterns as will your customers. Do you work from home and have contractors? This doesn't excuse you from this drill. In fact, you may have a greater challenge on your hands. With your partner on the other side of the city or across the seas, you may have to push harder to find that successful fulfillment strategy. Think about the impression it leaves on a potential buyer to see that your company runs seamlessly on systems right down to the music station playing in your office and while on hold. What does that say about your level of commitment? Still think this is a waste of time? If you take even the smallest of chores seriously, what will someone deduce about your ability to fulfill a promise? How's that for value added?

Exercise 3A.2

How will you share and implement Your Zen Way? Great job on doing your homework: you ought to be bursting at the seams with a full dose of your ways. You now need a method to let your team and other partners know about what you've been cooking up. They need to receive this news from you, Your Zen Way.

What are the new changes in procedures and why are they important? What about them afford an edge in the marketplace? What do you consider to be an advantage? You can use email and send it in stages, followed by a Q&A, but that's just one example. What unique method will ensure that your team knows and employs your way quickly? Start small if you need to. There are only so many hours in the day, and it's imperative that you still run your daily operations. But keep this exercise at the forefront of your to-do list. This is the type of planning that makes or breaks your future growth.

Systematic details are important and you have the power to control them. If a new contractor understands Your Zen Way and follows your recommendations, you've found somebody that supports your vision. What would you expect your customer to say after a go with your service? Conversely, what if your new contractor graciously passes on employing your way? What would be the impact on your customer retention rate if you and your contractor have a different way of operating? Would it increase? Or perhaps, decrease? However laborious these drills may appear, it's still far less work than finding a new client. Remember, you have a commitment to your customer. A promise to deliver your widget as advertised in Your Zen Code. You must have all of your team behind you pulling the same direction, your way. Your Zen Way has now been set and shared with your team, your customers, your partners, now it is onto Your Zen Pattern.

MOVEMENT 5: YOUR ZEN PATTERN

Think about the times you've borrowed or rented a car. Most of us never consider the planning that goes into a vehicle's interior for example. Aside from where the gas tank or electric plug is located, you probably don't think twice about hopping in, plopping your green tea between the seats and driving to your destination. But what are the chances of this borrowed vehicle being the exact same make and model you own? Not likely. Does this evoke worry? You probably don't give it a second thought. Where is the driver's seat adjustment? Where is the wiper switch, the turn signal and the speedometer?

Fortunately, auto manufactures have made it their job to help you get into any vehicle and begin a seamless experience with the road. Decades of engineering have gone into something we don't even notice - a learning curve. Everything is where you'd expect it. You're off and running from the moment you step in. All this efficient standardization is a marvel and makes for a safe and efficient drive. Your business has an interior just the same. I'm sure your Zen brain can extrapolate the parallel with this analogy. So, are you engineering your workspace?

You'll never say the line, "We really don't have a procedure for that," right? Well, that line has a twin sister. And it goes something like this, "Ah, we really don't have a place for that." There is a direct correlation between the flow and layout of your workspace and the productivity you would hope to extract from it. Where do you keep your stapler? Where are the extra pens? Think of how efficiently your team would operate if they never had to inquire or hunt for the location of a particular item, ever. Time is money. Your goal is to find every way imaginable to make it. This includes making sure you don't lose any. You can recover millions in a business if you perfect the art of efficiency. How much time do you waste every day looking for something? How much time does your team waste? Multiply those figures together by the amount of annual work hours and you get a gold mine.

In the early stages of growth, you are creating as you go. First time business ownership is a bit of an experiment. Let one or two days of production go without some organization and the second law of thermodynamics will mosey in. The more uniform and intuitive you make your space, the faster you move your new staff or partners into action. Action equals production and the ever-important element of profitability. You are the leader and this means being a shining example for everyone to follow. This is your business and you must sing the praises of organization throughout your space. Using Zen reasoning, it's not hard to deduce that you also, by default, have a corresponding pattern. Yes, Your Zen Pattern, where you and uniformity come together.

What would happen if auto manufacturers didn't put intuitive patterning at the forefront of planning? How would you feel if you hopped in a car and had to search for everything? It would be frustrating as well as unsafe. From here forward, your offices will be set up with everything in exactly the same place. If your staff has seen your office, and you've employed Your Zen Pattern, then they should already know what their office looks like. If you keep your stapler on the left side of your desk, that's the winning strategy until further notice. From now on, every office you create will have a stapler on the left side of the desk, a place for everything and everything in its place.

Of course, all of this sorting, placing and patterning comes at a price. If you don't have the wherewithal to compartmentalize every square inch of your facility, you can employ one of humanity's failsafes. How do you navigate a supermarket you've never been to before? How many millions of drivers avoid potential accidents and work hand in hand with other motorists? You guessed it. Signs. It's amazing to think about the effective simplicity of this invention. With or without the use of modern navigational gadgets, a simple sign can lead those who are lost directly to their destinations. Isn't this almost Zen-like?

Now it's your turn. Time to transform your space into a powerhouse production center. Create whatever signs or patterns of signs you deem most efficient. Why not make category signs or arrange by task and make area signs? Signs will move your staff in and out of your workplace without that detrimental element - a learning curve. Instead of focusing on basic needs, such as where the stapler is, your staff can address the duties that make the company money. So congratulations! Your invitation into the Zen Monster hall of fame is just around the corner. Create Your Zen Pattern to start saving time and money.

Exercise 3B

Let's establish your own "rinse and repeat" systems. This is your moment to discover the priceless skill of "buying time." So how do you start? Spend a moment organizing your space just the way you want it. Make it picture perfect. Take a photo and start notating placements of items. What is your office pattern layout? What are your operational pattern layouts? Perhaps breaking patterns down into the categories of *communicative, productive,* and *preparative,* could be helpful. Have one of your team members work with you if you like. In the beginning, you might have the most experience with layout and how you want your workflow to operate. But as you scale, you should consider your team's input and create flows that make the most sense for those who perform the daily work, integrating your vision along the way.

What is your uniform way of taking notes? Where in the office do you place them? Who knows, one day you may lose a team member to new opportunities. But this may not cause as much of a blip on the radar as you might think. Why not? Project notes will be exactly where you expect to find them, in the exact order they need to be.

How easy will it be for a new staff member to keep momentum? How's that for *communicative patterning.*

Does your team require the use of unsightly bottles of solutions, dusting rags and other tools to perform their work? What could the *productive* patterning look like? Perhaps all this can be stowed neatly in a portable cabinet with labels. A place for everything and everything in its place. Need a second set of supplies for a new hire? Easy! Just rinse and repeat. The more you address, the more time you buy. Where is your desk in relationship to the walls? What items are on it and what items are stowed below it? Patterning the intricate details will pay dividends in the long run. Because every time you add a new member, you'll only need to rinse and repeat, saving you and your staff hours.

Don't have the luxury of installing cabinetry everywhere to house all your pattern ideas? It's understandable that you wouldn't. In the beginning, space challenges are par for the course. Welcome to, "being clever with your resources 101". These are the exact same hurdles Fortune 500 COOs negotiate every single day. Operational budgets or not, you will always be forced to be more efficient for the remainder of your business career. So get in the game with something. Create a *preparative* location for your inventory and label it according to chore or project types.

Do your best to find every way possible to pattern. Tackle one area at a time. Create milestones. Set realistic targets. Schedule a time to pattern with your staff or stay late a night or two and establish your patterns in peace and quiet. Just get yourself in the game and begin to set up your productive space. Make one change as soon as you can. Then test it with your staff. Get feedback. You need to be open-minded about how to achieve the goal of slowing down the clock of inefficiencies and balancing preferences. But unless you try out different configurations over time, you will never know what pattern is truly optimal.

MOVEMENT 6: YOUR ZEN REFLECTION

Your vibe is the key to growth. It is imperative you adorn your space with the very elements that drive your creativity from day one. You must include every possible facet of you within it. What is your favorite color? Does your day start with a positive affirmation? Are you partial toward a specific journal or special pen? These are the small touches you make to complete the experience for your employees and customers. When your office becomes a personal reflection of your dream, the potential for it to scale in a manner that is manageable by you, unfolds accordingly. Put some energy into those walls and let the space do some directing for a change.

As a business owner, you have, by default, adopted the responsibility of bearing the torch of success through all the challenges that come along. With the trials and tribulations you may encounter, this torch bearing responsibility can take its toll. The sad truth is that most business owners put themselves last on the list of personal renewal. They burn out from denying that which makes them tick, that which would refuel the soul. They find they don't have time for it.

Creating a Zen experience for your business despite all the day-to-day tasks requires a space that continues to direct when you can't. A space to help you return to a wholesome charged state prepared for the challenges that lie ahead. For the sake of the company, your staff, and your customers, you must enthusiastically wave the torch every day and continue to lead your growth. So why not make your organization vibrate with a Zen magic that upholds your promises when you need to take a break? Enter, your personal tool of renewal and direction – Your Zen Reflection.

With Your Zen Reflection in place your staff will continue to follow Your Zen Code and Your Zen Way, even when you aren't there 100 percent of the time. Consider it something in the way of a gentle tap on the shoulder, a reminder of what you stand for. Make your space an expression of you. Your Zen Reflection is the very art of creating an environment where your hopes, dreams, inspirational leaders, and reference material is all in plain sight, guiding you, guiding your staff and guiding your customers. The challenge is how to best convey Your Zen Reflection to yourself and others.

It is not as hard as it might appear. Do you have a favorite album that embodies the importance of the promises you made to your customer? Guess what, your company soundtrack just inherited a new album. Do you start your day at home with a positive affirmation that embodies a "think outside the box" mentality? You now have a new addition to your morning meeting routine. What creative leaders do you admire? What legends do you strive to emulate? Whatever speaks to you, this is part of your essence and Your Zen Reflection is meant to celebrate it.

Consider once again our symbolic poster and fashion it next to your desk, in areas throughout your facility and perhaps even on your website. Let's say the poster is of your favorite band. When you choose to hang this particular poster, your decision took into account the unique traits of the artists and why you were drawn to them. Your Zen Reflection embodies your vision while performing tasks at work. It allows you to set goals based on the philosophy of that band, artist or cultural leader you admire.

For example, if you run a delivery company and you value customer service, then you might infuse your workspace with quotes about service and connection. It's much harder to push customer correspondence tasks farther down the list when the image on the wall portrays a smiling someone administrating to the needs of another. It's up to you how this is done. It will take time to perfect Your Zen Reflection. Employing these cultural cues are the keys to inspiring your team as they strive to provide customer promises the way you would, whether or not you are accessible.

Feeling a little self-conscious about putting yourself out

there by sharing all that inspires you? This is very natural. Adorning your space doesn't need to create stress. Every business, like every business owner, is different. By Zen default, your business will scale in a way that is unique. Some business owners are solely focused on the generation of cash. The mere thought of spending time decorating an office only takes away from bringing in precious dollars. In that case, I would suggest a new company slogan such as "Money First." At the very least that key axiom should be included in the employee handbook. Every employee should know why the walls are stark white and void of décor. They need to know the reason behind the rhyme to follow your vision. All in all, it will do your staff, partners and potential customers good to get a taste of your value system from the start.

Is all this decorative hoopla just a fancy way to disguise a "man cave" or "she shed" at work? As good as this sounds, it's hardly the case. This section is about leveraging your space to start working in your stead. It is an avenue of escape from the repetitive routine of directing everyone all the time and an endless repetition of do's and dont's. From all these new integrations, you will begin an avalanche of action and productivity embodying your mission and your offering, one that perpetuates your vision. Still not convinced? I'll cite one more example.

Have you ever "dressed to the nines" for an occasion where you wanted to look your absolute best? How did this affect the way you conducted yourself? How did you feel? How did you act? How did you make decisions?

How did you perceive the world around you? Was it different than a day you spent in your comfortable sweats? Presentation is one of the most powerful and greatly underestimated, underutilized tools in the world of small business. It is often considered just something you do once everything else is done. This misunderstanding couldn't be more detrimental.

Would you go to a special business occasion with your suit in a backpack and put it on after you've conducted your negotiations? More than likely you will be planning about your attire and personal presentation long before gathering your notes. Imagine how much more effective you would be looking your absolute best. Presentation is one of the biggest directors of action, like it or not. So perhaps from here on out, you might think twice about leaving those walls stark white. If your facility is decorated in a manner that cultivates your vision, "dressed to the nines" as it were, your staff will perceive, think, and act in a manner that would be very different than you in your sweats. A solid presentation opens up the door to so many new ways of creating solutions and making decisions. Sharing Your Zen Reflection is far better than a pamphlet thrown on your staff's desk with a few rules to follow about customer service.

With even a modicum of care in your office presentation, you can help steer your staff in a way that will prove successful. There's no right or wrong way to execute this plan. Perform your changes in stages if you're feeling apprehensive. Put your Zenersity front and center.

Maybe it's a fresh coat of paint on the wall to celebrate the company color. Maybe a stereo system for that band's album is in order. Perhaps it's just a book of quotes to reference before each meeting. Your essence, and the adornment of your space with it, is paramount. How will you infuse your space with your aspirational references? Start putting that list together, follow through, and watch the Zen magic come alive.

Exercise 3C

How will you demonstrate Your Zen Code and its six Axioms? What will continue to teach your staff when you're not around. Through subtlety you can effectively direct the mood within your facility. Take a moment to review the Axiom categories below and ask yourself two questions: 1) What artists, musicians, leaders, countries, language, quotes, etc. would best represent what I now stand for? 2) How can I communicate it within our space whether it be tangible or just on this side of virtual?

Using the following list of inspirations, choose one or more items that best complement your six Zen Code Axioms and find Your Zen Reflection.

> **Inspirations:** Artist, style of art, musician, band, genre of music, author, country, culture, language; leaders, scientist, philanthropists, quotes, other

Zen Code Axiom #1 – Your Philosophy of "Take"
a) Choose your inspiration(s)
b) Determine how the attribute embodies your Axiom 1?
c) Decide how / where to integrate this into your work environment.

Zen Code Axiom # 2 – The definition of your finished product or service
a) Choose your inspiration(s)
b) Determine how the attribute embodies your Axiom 2?
c) Decide how / where to integrate this into your work environment

Zen Code Axiom #3 – Your singular promise to the customer
a) Choose your inspiration(s)
b) Determine how the attribute embodies your Axiom 3?
c) Decide how / where to integrate this into your work environment

Zen Code Axiom #4 – Resources you will consult when problem solving.
a) Choose your inspiration(s)
b) Determine how the attribute embodies your Axiom 4?
c) Decide how / where to integrate this into your work environment

Zen Code Axiom #5 – Your signature flair
a) Choose your inspiration(s)

b) Determine how the attribute embodies your Axiom 5?

c) Decide how / where to integrate this into your work environment

Zen Code Axiom #6 – Your inspiration to the world

a) Choose your inspiration(s)

b) Determine how the attribute embodies your Axiom 6?

c) Decide how / where to integrate this into your work environment

You just dove deep into Your Zen Code Axioms in the previous chapter and now this drill? Is there any end? Feeling overwhelmed? Don't worry. If you cannot complete the entirety of this drill in one sitting, then this is proof that you care enough not to rush the process. Consult your schedule or budget to determine what sort of discovery time is possible. Address it in stages to keep your sanity. Regardless, do it. Create efficient intuitive space layouts, themed work environments, and documented procedures, all your way. That is music to my ears.

These actions, often set aside, will catapult you into hyperspace productivity. Employing the practices of top-level scalability and creating highways of business traffic that no competitor could touch. A new handbook on how to apply posters in every cube? Check! Grandfathered into the Zen Monster Hall of fame? Check! You've created the perfect setting to foster the following of supporters you've been working so hard to achieve.

You've done the work, everyone has the same pens, matching journals, and some jazz music playing in the background. Regardless, something feels off. An uneasiness lingers. There's an awkward silence each time you take out the book of quotes before a meeting. You might start feeling a little self-conscious about this whole addressing of space. Why is this?

Let's start with the obvious. Instead of an open arms welcome, your staff is staring at you with raised eyebrows. They want answers. The walls are now blue and there's a scattered collection of images of musicians, scientists, and philanthropists covering them. Your customers want explanations too. Are you ready to take it all back, revert to the way things were? Well, pull yourself together because there's something greater on the other side of these challenges. You're being pushed way outside your comfort zone. You're probably feeling like there's a little too much "your way" within these walls.

Now may be time to face the bittersweet transition into what most call, CEO status. Did you think it would be different? Although we'd all like to think that being the "big cheese" is gravy, this is in fact what real leadership feels like. A position that has nothing to do with the best parking spot, but has everything to do with creating a space that screams your vision. It's not always going to be the easiest or most popular seat in the house. You have just moved into the space where movers and shakers live every day. This is the world of the most impactful CEOs you read about, the ones who have made huge contributions to the totality of our world's socioeconomic realms. These heroes had the strength to walk into the businesses they were nurturing, embellish it head to toe with their vision. They then faced the uncomfortable moments when their entire team wondered what was driving the policy changes. These legends dove deep into the culture, finessed every part of the organization, managed the integration of policies and documentation to create the mega businesses we look at with awe.

Bearing the torch of growth and responsibility is not always an easy pill to swallow. You've chose the path less traveled and you have a responsibility to your team and customers to provide the financial wherewithal to keep them happy and growing; to keep yourself happy and growing. This position of responsibility calls for levels of mental strength you never thought you had. It takes a concerted effort to make your vision a reality. But when you put Your Zenersity first, your leadership skills will shine brightly, in a very uniform, scalable, and sustainable way. But you have to be willing to crack a few eggs to make that perfect omelet. Being uncomfortable during the transition period is part of the process.

Sticking it through the documentation and systems addressing will be one of the most memorable and fulfilling efforts you will ever set out to accomplish. Your customers and team will have high respect for you when they see the results of your new creative scaling at work. Be proud of yourself and what you are about to accomplish. You will have officially admitted and committed to who you are to the world, to your employees and to your customers. Everything from here forward completely encompasses that dream in your mind where you are directing a massive organization. A Zen Space where your following of supporters are working in harmony to achieve your vision.

Chapter Take Aways

Your Zen Way is realized when you reflect upon and document the way you do things, establishing systems and consistency. Consider these strategies to help you find the way:

1. Take note of particular details
2. Start with small things
3. Notice trends that reflect you

Then teach it to your staff, contractors and other team members. Remember to pick a style of dissemination that speaks to you. Make it unique.

Your Zen Pattern helps you organize your business space in the way you like it and creates standardization throughout your business space. Use these suggestions to help you get there.

1. Take a photo and notate placements of items

2. Break things down into the categories of communicative, productive and preparative
3. Have one of your team members work with you
4. Use this as your new standard

Your Zen Reflection is all about where you find your inspiration and how to chose to share it with others. You create the culture and the brand identity to share with the world. To do this you must find the inspiration that complements each of Your Zen Code Axioms (Chapter 3). Search who or what inspires you, for example, artists, style of art, musicians, bands, music genre, authors, cultures, language, business leaders, scientists, philanthropists, quotes, etc. Then apply to Your Zen Code Axioms.

1. The reason for continually creating this business enterprise is "x"
2. Every part of my being, organization and staff is directed to "x"
3. For every sale that travels through my enterprise, above all else, I will uphold the following commitment to "x"
4. In the interest of keeping my customer promise, I will always retreat to "x" for crossroads decisions
5. I will employ and ensure that my environment always embodies "x"

6. My organization imbues the world with "x"

Once you have assigned an inspiration, follow up with attributes which embody each Axiom and how and where you plan to integrate these into your work environment. For example with posters, a book of quotes, wall color, other images, etc.

MIND YOUR GROWTH

A CLEAN MENTAL SLATE (OR PLATE) MAKES ALL THE
DIFFERENCE.

You've worked hard and now it's time for a scrumptious dessert. How about some cheesecake or Créme Brulée? Perhaps you fancy strawberries swirled in chocolate fondue? Whatever you decide, envision something magical and make it a decadent medley of sweetness on its way to your pallet. That first bite will be a blissful experience to be remembered for lifetimes to come. Is your mouth watering yet? I hope so. But we aren't done. It gets better. Let's not forget that by this stage, your standards will be much more demanding.

You're on the path to the Zen Side of Business Ownership and imagining from a perspective of product delivery congruent with the deeper unique inner workings that come with it. Meaning, whatever dessert you're dreaming up, it will no doubt have a few promises about taste to back it up. Perhaps even some attitude. Consider this sugar fantasy as utterly unprecedented on every level.

Close your eyes and imagine a waiter bringing it to your table on a beautiful covered silver plate. Waiting in anxious anticipation for the bliss that will unfold with that first bite.

The waiter slowly removes the cover ready to reveal the decadence you've been dreaming about. But, as the aroma sends your cognitive imaginings soaring, you are taken back. How can this be? Something is not right. Your small slice of heaven has been slapped onto a plate marred with leftover spaghetti and meatballs. It has been mushed and mashed and swirled into an unrecognizable glob. All the delicious ingredients are staring right at you begging for a moment with your taste buds. So why not give it a go? Should it matter how this amazing dessert is served?

You have a passion. A passion to establish something bigger than you. A legacy in the marketplace that will continue to support your hunger for creativity long after the final garnishes are in place. You plan to build an enterprise that affords the financial wherewithal to support future endeavors. Whether you are contemplating your next business idea with a cup of green tea in hand or mentoring young business owners, there's no doubt you are aiming all of your resources at an organization that will soon be your legacy.

This is where you are headed as a Zen protégé, towards a future where you enjoyably reap the results of your hard work. But creating a masterpiece of a profit center requires every ounce of mental fortitude you can muster. One hundred percent of your focus in full growth alignment with nothing left to chance. All this future planning can be quite the task. If you don't want your future to be a mixed and mashed unwieldy bundle of confusion, settle down at the table and listen. It's time to start learning how to present your thoughts in a way that will serve your financial decision-making.

How many philosophers, great thinkers, and scientists throughout history have been drawn into the web of endless hypotheticals of the mind and its capability? Lifetimes have been dedicated to the studies and theories of human potential. In these varying dissertations there is an apparent common thread that most would agree to; a fundamental theme that unifies the diverse study behind it. This universal common denominator should be no surprise. Ready?

Your mind is your greatest asset in business. It is ever powerful. Your complete awareness of the very universe we live in takes place within your mind. When led, directed and focused, it can accomplish seemingly impossible feats. As in, the task of creating the financial legacy of your dreams. Whether it's the conscious mind or the untapped super-powerful subconscious, your cognitive capability remains the most powerful tool known on this planet. And as the loyal servant it is, it needs concerted coaching to lead it to its target.

Don't run your business with one hand tied behind your back. See your journey for what it is - your first responsibility. You are perhaps truly beginning to see what types of deals will start to build your bank account. Attack those opportunities and don't be swayed. Get in the game with every bit of your mental being. Imagine your business future focused dead-set on your goals and no one to shake you from the target. This is a target you set, a target for the future of your business where your company is moving currency effortlessly and creating an organization that is truly profitable - Zen Element #2

You owe it to your staff, your customers, and yourself to ensure that you do everything to hit it. This includes making the time to serve your vision on a perfectly sparkling dish. There will be no shortage of distractions vying for your attention ready to taint your flavorful thinking, rendering it as ineffective as the example set before you. So let's move on to master our next Zen Movement, Your Zen Pillar of Focus

MOVEMENT 7: YOUR ZEN PILLAR OF FOCUS

There's infinite growth energy within you waiting to be unleashed. Your ability to find your way through the daily mush is one of the biggest determiners of a successful outcome. Just like the car example in the Preface, you have a destination to get to. You have a road trip to navigate. Don't get too caught up in the excitement and stress of it all, because when you allow yourself to get entangled in every drama coming your way, you could miss that all-important turn. Or worse, find the road ahead of you dead ends. Don't take your eyes off your road! This is not as hard as it sounds and we have forerunners who have already set the stage on this existential path to clarity.

It's interesting that those "secrets to success" are what the great achievers over time left with us. Shouldn't there be other important lessons that they felt compelled to share? Why then is this concept of "thoughts controlling outcome" the singularly most reinforced theme from history's most enlightened ancestors and inventors? Why is the connection between the mind and our subsequent experience continually stressed? It is fascinating that the concept of thoughts driving the future outcome of your life is repeated over and over and over. Maybe they had a point.

There's no doubt that most people display a cursory understanding of these mindful ideas, for they, like most universal truths, are intuitive. If this is the one recurring theme over time which the great masters stress, then it ought to be in our best interest to understand and master its application. With even the smallest mental effort you will begin to yield physical manifestations that are in alignment with your financial vision. Call it Zen's little gift to you. If one is truly creating a clean mental slate when plotting out future decisions, imagine how you, in full focused force, could bulldoze obstacles that lie ahead.

There are 101 ways for your ideas not to work and plenty of people to remind you of this fact. You need to focus on the one way it will. You need the mental clarity to push through and recognize when you are being tempted to veer from Your Zen Code or Your Zen Offering.

If your metaphorical serving plate needs to be pure as to not diminish the experience of the dessert it holds, so too is the relationship between your mindset and the decisions you make from it. Your mind is the platter on which you place all of the sorting, contemplating, and sifting of data from the senses. You then proceed to direct people, discuss options, and personally intend the future outcomes of your desires. If you have any extraneous scattered energies and thoughts distracting you while you're performing your decision making, you are more than likely getting skewed results similar to your dream dessert, served on a dirty plate.

We are all weighted down by the stresses of everyday challenges from work, family, finances, friends, community, ad infinitum. Well over half of your cognitive resources are tied up in these processes, cycles and stresses that come along with them. Left over spaghetti anyone? There's nothing wrong with juggling multiple duties. Do you think it's a healthy practice to make your business decisions in the middle of all that drama? Putting emergencies aside, you want 100 percent of your cognitive resources available when you are focused on your business. This is more important than you could ever imagine. Don't fall into the trap of taking your organizational decisions lightly.

Case in point, are you making a decision on a current project? Your mental state matters. Before you make that decision, you need to be sure to clean off the proverbial plate and stay true to the path that most serves your efforts. This is the sort of mental challenge you'd expect to see in every business poised for great things. It is nothing new to top business leaders. The best CEOs of our time understand the power behind this concept. Every day, they are challenged with decisions that determine the life and death of their financial future. Their success depends on holding strong to their set direction. Remember Zen Code Axiom #4? When everyone else is telling them the multitude of ways their idea won't work, there they are, trudging forward. When things waver, they hold their ground and push through.

Similarly, every part of your business creation will be challenged from day one. However uncomfortable it might make you, you are the one who will save the day. Take a closer look at the silver lining in this challenge. Your predicament is no different from so many in the business world. For every problem you are going to have is in some way, shape, or form, the same problem that Fortune 500 CEOs encounter in their roles. True, they can delegate, and maybe you can't. But the word delegate implies that they know what to do. They have to be able to gauge the solution and put in place the appropriate counter measures, just like you.

Don't brush off your responsibility as anything short of what it truly is. Give your position the credit it deserves. Start making the time to put your destination front and center. You are a Zen Machine, one that holds together when everything around begins to challenge you or perhaps fall apart. While this sounds like a nearly impossible task, with a little help from one of your new Zen Movements, this decision-making role just got a whole lot easier.

Welcome in, Your Zen Pillar of Focus. You will now be directing your cognitive capability to work from a place of fortitude, a mighty pillar, one that deliberately discerns what's in your field of decision-making daily and making hard choices, one that stands tall in the face of challenge.

What does the deployment of Your Zen Pillar of Focus entail? Is it a magic wand to wave at everything stressful only to have it all vanish in thin air? In some ways, it is. Just like all of your Zen Movements, it's surprisingly simple and effective. You are going to become the world's best sorter. From now on, all interruptions will go into a set of Zen bins to be reviewed, four specific bins to place each and every distraction that comes your way. Each to be handled at a later time. Can you hazard a guess at what those bins might be titled? Well, try this on for size: What constitutes operating from the Zen Side of Business Ownership? It encompasses four qualities, right? It is an enterprise that 1) embodies you, 2) affords prosperity, 3) creates a following of supporters, and 4) serves a community of people. Congratulations, you've just named your bins. Each corresponds to one of your four Zen Elements and should look like the following:

Bin #1) Issues that compromise your embodiment or aspects of Your Zenersity.
Bin #2) Issues that encroach on your profitability.

Bin #3) Issues that disrupt the harmony of your loyal
supporters and team.
Bin #4) Issues that stifle your service to the community
and customers

At every moment of every day, direct each concern to
the appropriate bin and address it later only when your
mental slate is spic and span. You have Your Zen Code to
reference and you have your bins. When you run into an
entanglement, write it down and categorize it to the
appropriate bin. Is your customer unhappy about the
product you've delivered? Immediately do everything you
can to remedy the situation, but when all is said and done,
write down the complaint and place it in bin #4. What
about a financial issue? Did the price of the parts you use
to make your widgets go up? Write it down and place it
where? That's right, bin #2. Is there a disagreement among
your team? That will be in bin #3 please. When things
quiet down, address the bins in an order that makes the
most sense for you. Maybe it takes a few weeks to solve a
problem. Maybe it happens in a few minutes. The solution
to your increased costs could be as simple as absorbing
them if you have the wherewithal restructuring your
pricing. Maybe it's time to look at new suppliers or
renegotiate with your current one.

Realistically these bin lists may accumulate fast. But
don't feel defeated. You will feel empowered with the new
information you are uncovering. These are areas to
improve your business, ways that help you become the

leader you were born to be. Does your team disagreement stem from a lack of instruction and a standardization that a refined Zen Pattern could solve? These are the solutions that you must dig deep to uncover. You can only tackle these decisions when you've had a chance to let the dust settle from the day to day, when Your Zen Pillar of Focus is fully engaged.

There is much more behind the exercise of being a leader who knows when it's time to sort and when it's time to address. Without a balance between day to day operations and the general improvements you need to make, your business will not sustain the growth it's trying its hardest to achieve. This type of discernment takes practice. Do you always feel the need to immediately solve every problem that comes in? Why is this? Could the answer simply be a misunderstanding of what success really means for a growing organization?

As business owners we've been trained to think that the only indicator of success is the top line sales column or expressions of it. "My business grosses this much", "I've doubled my staff," or "We've secured so many new clients." SUV seats anyone?

But this isn't you anymore. You've found this book because you've been seeking a new definition of success - a Zen holistic approach. If you are completing the drills set out in this book, you will be on the Zen Side of Business Ownership and running a perfectly well-oiled machine that fuels itself and moves you forward. Lean on these teachings and foundations as the assurance that you are on the right track.

You must be realistic about the progress you hope to see from your new modus operandi. Things won't change overnight. But if you stay the course you'll feel the shift every night you take out your bins and design a strategy to handle the issues within them. Stop worrying about your success and the need to challenge everything in your field of vision. You are already doing things perfectly. Just summon Your Zen Pillar of Focus, write it down and begin to savor the flawlessly plated dessert of your dreams.

Exercise 4A

Assign a diary, digital list or some form of recording device to keep with you at every moment of the business day for bin assignments. When you reach a kink or upset, write it down in one of your four bin categories. As you experience less than desirable moments in day-to-day operations, take note of what needs addressing, things that stand out to you. Did a customer leave unsatisfied? Write it down. Did your staff forget to put the special toppings on the cake? Make a note and move on. What else is bothering you? Not enough time away to have a life? Write down these concerns and place them in the appropriate bin. Remember, each bin corresponds to one of your four Zen Elements and should look like the following:

- **Bin #1)** Issues that compromise your embodiment or aspects of Your Zenersity.
- **Bin #2)** Issues that encroach on your profitability.
- **Bin #3)** Issues that disrupt the harmony of your loyal supporters and team.
- **Bin #4)** Issues that stifle your service to the community and customers

Exercise 4B

Assign a time to go over your bins and address the issues. Sit down, without distractions, and begin to look at all the notes you've composed. Is it once a day? Is it once a week? Or is it at the end of a project? The decision is completely up to you, but you must make it a part of your routine. Some issues will need addressing sooner than others and it will serve you well to ensure that detrimental concerns are put at the top of the list. But all categories are integral on the Zen Side of Business Ownership and should have a realistic resolution date or milestone. Don't procrastinate too long on clearing your bins.

Conversely, do not try to solve all of your problems in one sitting. You will go crazy if you do. Quality wins over quantity in the Zen world. If you put too much on your plate, (pun intended) you will be back to a dirty plate. You have to be present for all the action in the day to day. You have a business to run. Don't rush those very precious planning moments to see results quickly. Take the right amount of time to establish the solutions that align with everything you've put in place. Don't be discouraged if this takes more practice than you anticipated. You may be breaking routines you've been at for years. Regardless of the mental break-in period, simply going through these steps puts you on the track to success. You have to begin the process. When's it going to be? Decide right now as to the ever-important time of review.

Has this been just a work "on" the business versus work "in" the business argument, a plan to delegate your time? Hardly. Keeping a clear head for planning and decision-making can mean the life or death of your business. Being the person responsible for the growth of an organization is one of the most challenging ventures one can ever undertake. There is no set formula; just accepted practices at best. Every business is different. Therefore, winning strategies to overcome growth setbacks vary accordingly. These formidable facts and figures are powerless against you now that you have a way to address them.

You are a Zen Pillar of Focus, working like the best of the top CEOs. Although you aren't on this earth to gain approval from folks farther along the business path than you are, you would do well to enjoy a comparison here and there as a reminder that you are operating like the best of them. It's not unhealthy to give yourself a pat on the shoulder for just how far you've come. There's still plenty to do and you need to stay positive moving forward. You will have to wield Your Zen Pillar of Focus not just once, not just twice, but every day, all of the time. So don't fall into the dirty dish cycles of stresses, doubts and problems about whether or not you are running a tight operation.

Every day you are cutting through clutter and making a smooth-running machine, keeping a cool head and filling up those bins. This is real leadership - removing obstacles that are not in the best interest of your business before they have the chance to wreck havoc and doing so with calculated adjustments one at a time in peace and quiet.

You possess the mental strength to create a space and time where you can carefully gauge the problems of your daily operations and put in place the correct counter measures. You are taking the helm and leading your business's growth. Your customers are depending on you to grow. Your team is depending on you to grow. Your bank account is ready to grow. So go ahead, lift off that cover and enjoy your decadent dessert. Be sure to send your compliments to the chef and to you, for the clean and beautiful plate it was served on.

Chapter Take Aways

Your Zen Pillar of Focus provides you with a solid and true ability to decipher what matters now and what can wait for your attention. It serves as an invaluable tool as you approach your leadership role and address your administrative responsibilities. Use Your Zen Pillar of Focus to solve systemic problems and finesse your vision for smooth and successful operations. As challenges emerge, write them down and assign them to categories (bins) based on the elements defined in the Zen Side of Business Ownership (Preface/Chapter 1). Be sure to set aside a regular time to consult your bins and address issues before they become crises.

- **Bin #1)** Issues that overstep your embodiment or aspects of your Zenersity
- **Bin #2)** Issues that encroach on your profitability
- **Bin #3)** Issues that disrupt the harmony of your loyal supporters and team
- **Bin #4)** Issues that stifle your service to the community and customers

INITIATE CONTACT

TIME TO BE THE SUPERHERO YOU WERE BORN TO BE.

"Captain Connect To the Rescue!"

To the Rescue! Do you remember that hero call, hollering it again and again as your childhood super hero came to the aid of those in distress. The familiar line you cried out to the universe; to those unfortunate souls on the precipice of the perilous void of boredom, solitude and disconnect. Here to the rescue is Captain Connect, the superhero built into every child's psyche, dazzling countless fragmented souls into safety with the cunning ability to story tell, share and explore. By night, you were just another seemingly ordinary human, sleeping and dreaming as a mere child. Nobody could have suspected the creative skills that lurked beneath. But by day, you morphed into a radiant guru connecting with all those close to you.

Captain Connect to the rescue. Saving the world with

the power of the childhood Zenersity you didn't know you had. Touching those around you with the latest and greatest adventure you were cooking up. Right there with a new skill to show-off or a story to share. With every informative broadcast, came wonder and appreciation from those destined to be rescued. Those potentially caught in the throes of the evil forces of separatism and non inclusion. Each distress call snuffed out quickly. That was you, a sharing superhero. Calling out for hours just to present a new creation and the lost souls in your world loved you all the more for it.

Does the above bring back some heroic nostalgia from your childhood days? Do you recall saving victims who may have been in the depths of disconnect? Or did you think you were just a regular old kid? It's understandable if this superhero title you earned as a child is news to you. Within all of life's bustles, a formal coronation ceremony probably never made the calendar. But no matter, the connections you made and the sharing you did were nothing short of miraculous and worthy of commending. On behalf of the world, I say thank you, for your hard work and efforts. Saving the universe every day with your incessant tugging and pulling at those around you for attention to be paid with the currency of connection, to want nothing more than to let an experience express itself through you.

Let us celebrate the Captain Connect legacy, because we all inherited this heroic reputation at some point or another in our early career. Whether you shared a song you learned, a toy house you built or a drawing that captured your pet perfectly, you stopped at nothing to ensure those around you knew about the great creation that took place. Perhaps it was a cake you baked or a laugh with friends. Maybe even a time you recited a story for your classmates, you couldn't help but share it with everyone around you. Your unknown objectives were to have a genuine moment with someone, to be your best, and bring people closer to you. Simply wanting to enjoy your gifts and talents with folks you cared about.

Now, fast-forward to mature present day business you. Are you still as genuine and eager to disseminate every part of your truest being to those who would most benefit? Or have you abandoned your childhood cape and replaced it with a more marketable mask? Have the innocent days been replaced by accepted trends; swapping "connection" with "pushing outreach" and "leveraging" hoping to brush shoulders with somebody in the process? There's nothing wrong with outreach and creating an impression in the marketplace. This entire chapter is devoted to ensuring you achieve this. Shining your offering light is paramount if you hope to expand your business beyond your initial circle of customers.

Has connection for you become just a game of amassing endless lists of contacts and driving conversion, up selling and choosing this word over that to garner the winning title of most popular? Perhaps it's time to change your approach and address the deeper fulfillment of initiating contact; one that you perfected innately as a child. Inside you is an inherent necessity to express your truest passions and connect with those who would most be inspired to share in all the fun; a desire to unleash the passions for genuine exchanges that drove you to start your business in the first place!

Maybe it's time to pull out your old glittery superhero cape and become the grown-up Captain Connect you were meant to be. Because without your purest most radiant light of an offering front and centermost, people will continue in oblivion. You'll risk them falling into the depths of monotony and stagnation with no one to gift them with the creative diversity only you can deliver. They will be left to live unfulfilled lives without the precious puzzle piece that is you tugging hard on their sleeve.

What is initiating contact in the sense I'm advocating? It is letting your truest light be known to the ones you choose. It is the process of introducing the offering you've worked so hard to achieve to the like-minded consumers who will get on board. It is showcasing your truest Zenersity for what it is. While some might refer to this as marketing 101, initiating contact transcends many of the modern day belief systems held within advertising and outreach. It is allowing your idiosyncratic, Zenergistic, quirk-tastic side to be the guiding light to future connections. It's addressing an entirely different spectrum of customer outreach that will have you bringing in those who will look to you as the hero you are. It is sharing your offering in a fashion that creates the connections leading you straight to one of the most fulfilling components on the Zen Side of Business Ownership - creating a following of supporters - Zen Element #3

MOVEMENT 8: YOUR ZEN TAP

Beautiful examples of humanity's desire for human contact and subsequent connection can be witnessed across the planet. A brief glimpse would reveal an abundance of digital mediums, social constructs, and communities all aimed at this very task. Avenues that afford reach and visibility to every part of this world are designed for the sole purpose of establishing a lasting bond. A business can garner visibility in a heartbeat by connecting with new customers overnight like never before. Through these continuous developments, the number of souls, or should I say, potential buyers, ready to engage your services compounds daily.

Organizations from all ends of the earth are now able to search out and find like-minded individuals in virtually every segment at light speed. The odds of success are in your favor. It's a great time to get your new offering out there. Scooping up a potential buyer is as easy as pushing your old trusty x-ray button. But be careful. Is this dominating crusade for market share the beginning of a Zen-biotic relationship? Should you fire that laser beam at every soul making your call to heroism just a helter-skelter attempt to snatch the totality of everyone in sight, whether or not they want what you have to offer?

Your business needs fuel to run and there's no doubt

your operation is thirsty for growth. But there's no need to squeeze into guises that don't reflect your truest offering just to check off a marketing list of "to-dos". Things operate very differently within the parameters of a system that celebrates Your Zenersity. Look at who you've become including all the momentous growth and experience you represent in the marketplace. You have solidified Your Zen Offering, cracked Your Zen Code, and developed Your Zen Way. These are not things to be taken lightly and indeed must reach your potential customers. These are the foundations that will support the lasting connections you've been searching out from day one; your singular promise, your commitment to delivery. Do you have the confidence to step onto the marketplace ledge with your undiluted sharing cape in hand?

Calling all superheroes! Calling all superheroes!
Initiate "Connect" sequence immediately!

Being that grown-up Captain Connect in the business world comes with a few stresses, I mean responsibilities. On one hand, you have the sands of time running through the hourglass, and on the other, costly operations to keep the doors open. It's expected that you will feel pressure to perform the seemingly impossible with the constant mantra of "time is ticking" in your ear. There's a finite window in which to establish the necessary resources to fuel the expense column staring at you daily. The need to fulfill your financial obligations is the driver for many of the decisions you make. Often it is the leading impetus for the marketing and outreach efforts you undertake. If ever there was a time to employ Your Zen Pillar of Focus, it's now.

So blast the word out. The urge to pull out the advertising laser and fire it across the marketplace skyline is at the top of your to-do list. Fire! Fire! Fire again! Is there a connection or two to be had on the other side? Just get some business in the door. But is casting a broad net and reaching out really the answer? Is the ever-powerful "Fire When Ready" method what you want to deploy to attract the customers to whom you want to connect? Perhaps it's time to explore a gentler alternative. I propose that a nice light Zen Tap on the shoulder is a better solution.

Of course, we see Fortune 500 superheroes "Fire" all the time. The exuberant launches and national campaigns calculated to the fifth decimal point for return. There is a little more to that story than meets the eye. Something you should understand about the massive advertising efforts around you is that as consumers what we see as the finished commercial is just a sliver of the action. A zany 30 second advertisement, a heart wrenching story, or a celebrity speaking sincerely; all of these are aimed at delivering a message to consumers to be remembered for all time. The sole purpose is to accomplish the crucial task of securing cashflow for the next quarter. This should be no surprise to you. You're a business owner after all.

What we, as consumers, don't see in these impressive campaigns is the hours and hours of formulaic surveying, case studies, story boarding and strategic planning all geared to help our Fortune 500 hero do one thing with its lost souls. Something you perhaps already perfected as a child – connect with them. Countless dollars are spent creating the very phenomenon you perfected as a kid. The very skill you were given at birth.

You already possess the solution that will turn your sales stresses around, hightailing them far out of sight. So why then do we reach for the marketing laser gun every time? The unfortunate deception in this cloudy world of outreach is that the zany tale, the endorsement, or the compelling story is the very thing that will fuel your business; the prized effort to bring the sales and connection you've been seeking. But take it from our Fortune 500 heroes, the portion of the campaign visible to the consumer is a small part of the magic.

Real connection starts with identifying your lost souls. Understanding their needs, and realizing you are the superhero that can save them. Knowing thyself through and through, understanding your own needs and how you'd like to be saved is key. It's time to put your ray gun back on the shelf and begin to carefully sow the seeds of a lasting bond using your own passions. While this might entail further self-discovery, not defining your lost souls could be a far greater loss for both you and them.

Is outreach and connection the same thing? Many confuse the two in the context of marketing. As business owners it can be all too easy to think one equals the other. To draw a clear distinction, within the group-set of outreach exists a clear category of connection and this is what you are targeting. Creating a presence in the marketplace is integral to the life cycle of a business. One way or another you will have to engage customers through a form of outreach; to let potential patrons know you exist and that you are ready to serve them up something wonderful. How this is accomplished is your unique responsibility to discover. It's a direction focused entirely around connection. Don't feel pressured to pursue advertising efforts that don't speak to you for the sake of perceived outreach. Often the best connection opportunities are right at your feet.

Our plant and animal kingdom is full of the harmonious connections to inspire you. The Earth is a beautiful macrocosm of experience which affords every imaginable creation its inhabitants can muster up. Every plant and animal depends on another. Species work together, perfectly. There is the ultimate connection. Flowers lean on the symbiotic interactions of nature's insects and birds to procreate. The growth and survival of each species can be seen in perfect Zenchronicity; taking only that which is needed and leaving that which is not; growing in number whether in packs or clans, plant kingdoms or the insect world, working in harmony with each other. There's no such thing as a shotgun approach or a fingers crossed mentality for connection on planet Earth.

Not doing things in just the right order is the difference between life and death in the animal kingdom. Does the tiger jump at everything moving before it or does it study its market? As nature's inhabitants often do, it calculates everything to the highest degree. Checking off one by one from the list of criteria: not too big, not too small, not too fast, not too slow. The tiger instinctively assesses its perceived ability to single out and tackle a given subject. It's only then, when all dials align perfectly, that it leaps.

Does a blooming flower need every bee from around the world to pollinate it to thrive? Similarly, reaching your lost souls doesn't mean making sure your offering is heard through the galaxy in its totality. Ambitious outreach targets are always encouraged, but remember quality wins over quantity in the Zen world. Our thriving flower only needs a specific set of bees performing a specific task in a specific order over a specific period of time to expand its legacy.

Operating on the Zen Side of Business Ownership is not a popularity contest of who can garner the most attention through powerful outreach. You are a small business and have limited resources both financially and logistically. One perfect tap on the shoulder to just the right group, in just the right way, at just the right time equals a perfect save for both you and them. Stay true to every form Your Zen Code dictates. These are your rules. These are your people. How you save them from disconnect is up to you.

A Fortune 500 superhero's triple laser blast of marketing utilizes mainstream mediums to achieve the desired goals. But what about using your new Zen Code which is there right in front of your hero boots? It is Your

Zen Code that encompasses the methods which speak to your heart, methods born from your passions. You are striving for connection, not outreach. While connection and outreach work hand in hand, understanding the relationship between the two is the make or break for filling your contact list with lasting supporters.

What will you say? How will you say it? What pain point are you solving? Fortunately, you don't have to drag yourself through hours and hours of discovery because you've already done the work. The answers are right there in Your Zen Code and with a bit of development on each, you will be one step closer to being that Captain Connect you were as a kid.

What would stop you in your tracks and make you want to do business with yourself? Celebrating the very things you stand for, of course. If you don't show off a little of Your Zen Code, the very things you stand for, how can you expect your customer to connect with it?

Consider, if you were lost in a crowd looking for what your business has to offer, what would you want to hear? Is it the ubiquitous, "My product is the best!" or, "My product is the cheapest!" What would turn your head? If you're selling chairs and want to celebrate creativity, then your Zen Code Axiom # 2 (Your Product) write up might begin with the line, "The chair that inspires you to think outside the box." Whammo! Did you see heads turn? Or how about a write up featuring Your Zen Code Axiom #6 (Your Contribution). Your campaign tagline might be,

"One idea is all it takes to change the world." You just saved of bunch of somebodies.

Where should you disseminate your message? Ask yourself, where would you want to hear that message. Where are the people who benefit from what you have to offer? Search deep. Ask yourself, where do you spend your time? Perhaps this is where your lost souls seeking connection might be. Hero time!

See the difference? Does this method call for the abandonment of digital mediums? On the contrary, you should have great follow up and consistency everywhere. It's not an either/or mentality. Express yourself in as many places that Your Zen Code write-ups lead you. You have much to be proud of and show off. Having a presence in every place possible makes you more accessible when your lost souls are drawn your way. But always remember, connection is your driving force.

Exercise 5A

Refer to each of your six completed Zen Code Axioms from Chapter Two. Address and reflect upon each of these beautiful guiding light statements one at a time. (They should look like the sentences below.)

1. The reason for continually creating this business enterprise is:_____

2. Every part of my being, organization, and staff is directed to:_____

3. For every sale that travels through my enterprise, above all else, I will uphold the following commitment: _____

4. In the interest of keeping my customer promise, I will always retreat to _____ to be the guiding light for crossroad decisions.

5. I will employ and ensure that my environment always embodies: _____ as a defining component and identity to which my company, staff, contractors, and other partners will universally uphold.

6. My organization imbues the world with: _____.

Place each statement separately before you. Write one or two paragraphs on why it is important to you. How does it bring the consumer a greater experience? How does it help overcome a set of unique problems? How is it revolutionary? These are your words, your exploration. Anything you come up with is perfect. This is your chance to explain your case, in your own unique Zen Way.

Exercise 5B

Now take each one of your new Zen Code write-ups and deeply reflect on each one. Decide where that message best resonates with you. How should you communicate it to the world? It could be digital mediums and inspirational blasts or perhaps tangible postings. Possibly it could be conveyed through trainings or business to business trade shows involving in-person handshakes. You decide.

Write, rewrite and assign new areas of dissemination to your heart's content. Continually rediscover methods of connection. Because if I ask you, "What group of people want to know about your offering most?", and your answer is "everyone," then you're still reaching for the old ray-gun and need to dig deeper. Be explorative and push your creativity. Take your time.

The more personal and intimate you design Your Zen Tap to be, the more likely it is that you will form a firmly solid connection and yield a much higher return. You will create a following of supporters and strengthen your business. You will be on the Zen Side of Business Ownership! Most importantly, you will begin to hear feedback and inquiries that are very different. You won't have the usual questions such as "What do you do?" Or, "Explain again what you make?" Perfecting your best Captain Connect strategy ensures that only those who need what you have will begin to be drawn to you. Instead of the same old questions, you'll start hearing things like, "I love what you're doing." Or I'm so glad somebody finally provides this level of service." Or, even better, "I love that you're making a difference." All the while handing over their dollars in appreciation of your offering. You have connections to make, meaningful ones. As you begin to sew the new seeds of connection, get ready. Once you perfect Your Zen Tap and display it in front of the ones you choose, heads will turn. When they do, you need to be ready. Ready to tackle them with your offering, I mean, a very Zen-like tackle, I call it the Zen Pounce.

MOVEMENT 9: YOUR ZEN POUNCE

It's time to stand tall over the precipice of the marketplace, Captain Connect! Part Two of this superhero adventure is every bit as powerful as the first. You've done your homework, summoned those lost souls with a clever tap on the shoulder, impressed them with your passionate contributions and your solemn promise. Now, they are walking your way filled with curiosity, moving in to get a better look. As you triumphantly gaze at the city below and watch formerly lost souls now jumping with enthusiasm, you have the opportunity to create something special. You've accomplished something all companies would stop at nothing to achieve - connections for life, or as they say in the industry, promoters. They are coming to you. These are customers who sing your praises long after they left. They gather other like-minded individuals and return to your establishment in greater numbers, turning two customers into four, four into eight, eight into sixteen and on and on. You are set up to make this happen.

But you must now wield the Zen Movement that will evoke such a state; making your customers feel like they've made it home, embrace them with open arms. They are drawn to what you stand for and want to be part of the magic you've created. It's like finding long-lost friends who you are ready to welcome home. Even though not one dollar has exchanged hands, they have perhaps already bought into your product simply in support of you. Be ready with the tool that will solidify the connection; something born from your passions to instill the very same enthusiasm you've had for your business from day one. Time to employ Your Zen Pounce, one of the sharpest tools in your box.

Springing in for the embrace with something only you can give them, that's Your Zen Pounce. It is a sign; a special gift to celebrate their return; something that leaves an emotional imprint on them forever. Think back to the tiger seeing its prized possession. Watching with wide eyes, crouching low, digging in its hind legs until just the right moment, and then, the pounce, leaping in full force with the entirety of its being.

This is you, leaping in and rescuing with the entirety of Your Zenersity. You must spring to action when you engage your services, pounce with everything you've got, and never let go. Solidifying the sharing moment with a gift that transcends time itself. So go ahead, channel your inner tiger.

Is all this gratuitous brouhaha and excitement for somebody walking through the door really in order? You may be thinking, "Can't I just hand them a balloon, a free mint or say 'Thanks' for coming?" Not even close. Until you realize that sharing and deep connection is the key to making great waves in your industry and business, you'll just be spinning your outreach wheels.

Creating Your Zen Pounce means looking deeper to discover the gift that will complete your new customer's experience. Does a tiger put half its effort into the chase and end up with the prize? Nature does not work that way and neither will you. Creating a following of supporters means going all in. Remember, you have a promise to deliver. You've invested so much into your organization and now it's down to the final pounce. Just like a tiger, you won't pounce on everything crossing your path. This particular Zen movement is intended for those special folks who see you for the hero you are. (Don't worry, there's an entire chapter to come which is devoted to the very identification process that helps you spot your chosen ones.) But if this person has found their way to you, it's an occasion worth celebrating, worth rewarding, worth pouncing on.

In your history as a consumer, there may perhaps be a handful of times you felt truly special from a business exchange. Was it a time you received a special tour or VIP treatment of sorts? Maybe it was a special preparation of your favorite drink by a bartender who remembered your name. Regardless, it was an experience where time stopped and it was clear that life was all about the little things. These are moments of lucidity in the seemingly viscous world of commerce, moments of true sharing. Times when you deeply connected with a product or service so much so that it continued to resonate with you long after the purchase. A deeper relationship was evident and you felt less like just another number and more like someone special. The moment you knew you found something worth supporting, something that really got you.

When you recall those times, do you describe them using words such as conversion and leverage? Of course you don't. Terms such as these lose their appeal in the Zen world where sharing is the kingpin of business transactions. Think back, how did that sharing experience and connection continue to express itself? Did you relive it over in your mind or share the story with others.

Connection is a very powerful tool. It is one of the few things we as Earth's inhabitants innately strive to achieve and have the power to create. Imagine the effect you will have in the marketplace, in your local community and on your new partners. This is not about just handing over a free widget. True sharing is apparent in the little things, the details.

Your Zen Pounce is about creating a way for your customers to experience the passion you have for your business, naturally bringing you together. Having them walk away with a spring in their step and a smile on their face knowing they can count on you; making a solid connection with your product or service. Imagine, your customer positively recalling the experience of doing business with you, telling friends about it and anxiously waiting for the next opportunity to work with you again. You can achieve this. You already have the toolset.

Ask yourself this, "What will leave a mark on them forever?" Focus any aspect of your six shiny Zen Code Axioms directly at your customers. Is it an impromptu tour with backstage photo opportunities of the magic behind your craft? Is it a plaque on the wall that bears their name? Is it a small book you wrote on your craft or a special take away "Thank you" poster? What object, gesture or service, when placed in the hands of your customer would demonstrate that you do actually "get" them? More than likely it is the very thing that would "get" you. Don't worry about whether something is too small. If this something is truly born from your heart, it will be evident and whatever you decide will be perfect.

Exercise 5C

Take a moment to reflect on what your business means for the world. What are you helping to create? Perhaps look to Zen Code #6 (Your Contribution) for inspiration. How can you package it as a token of thanks, that moment of pure connection, a reminder to your customer that there's something bigger happening between the exchange. Write down something you can produce easily, hand over, speak, or deliver in some fashion to your customer. It should be something that reflects the values and beliefs of you, the one person with the Zenersity who drives the company. The important thing is that customers walk away from the experience knowing they've found someone who "gets" them. Write it down and start creating the lasting relationships that have been waiting for you for too long.

Attention all superheroes! Attention all superheroes! Crisis Averted! Sharing and connection have triumphed!

So now, you're standing at the ledge of the marketplace with the keys to unlimited potential in your belt and your heroic cape waving triumphantly in the wind. A shiny suit with your solemn promise displayed for all. Your beautiful Zen Movements at your side. Take a good look at yourself, hardly camouflaged in the guises of conformity. From top to bottom, you are a master of connection. You're a sharing force to be reckoned with, a majestic figure above the marketplace. The super sharer you've always been. Making connections in a way that only you can.

And what will you do from here? Hopefully, blast your light into the sky signaling your presence and then get ready to pounce. You can now shift outreach paradigms with your pinky and move saving practices ever so slightly into a space where close connection is focused squarely at creating lasting bonds between buyers and sellers. There's a new contagious drive to put customers and relationships first. I can already feel a sense of ease and loyalty in the city. The evil forces of solitude have been swept out of sight. Amazing! We have you to thank. You've created a place where connection is the corner stone of every person who walks through your door; a place where people come first. On behalf of the world, I say thank you. For all those who continue to make connection your driving force, I also say thank you! Finally, to those cutting through the churn and burn and upholding a future where super sharing can be found around every corner, I have one thing to say, "The world is a better place with you, Captain Connect!"

Chapter Take Aways

Your Zen Tap; Make an effort to determine how each of Your Zen Code Axioms is important to you. Spend the time to think long and hard and be thorough. Then decide where that message will best resonate with the world. Once you have discovered your Zen Tap, you will have established your target market and explored the many avenues of marketing and customer connection to benefit your business.

Your Zen Pounce is your clincher, your time to come in with all you have. Package one of Your Zen Code Axioms into a token of thanks to your customer to create a moment of pure and lasting connection. The end result of a powerful Zen Pounce? Repeat business and additional referrals.

BUILD STRONG ROOTS

STEADY GROWTH COMES AT A COST. IS YOUR CUSTOMER
PREPARED TO PAY IT?

Y ou are tasked with fixing a nagging plumbing leak. You don't actually mind a trip to your local hardware store confident that Bill, the owner, will come to your aid. He knows a lot more about DIY than you and always takes the time to help. Despite the problem on your hands, you cheer up knowing that he will walk you through the process and say those magic words, *"This is exactly what you need. If you run into trouble just call me."* Plumbing disaster averted. Bill is the best.

You spend time and energy problem solving your own business issues all week long and the last thing you need is another challenge to negotiate on the weekend. Thankfully you have Bill, the once-contractor turned business-owner, with his magical shop of specialty parts, widgets, thingamabobs, and whatchamacallits. His resident dog, Sparky, is always there to greet you at the door. They are like family. You drive up to the parking lot, stop and look in, but something's not right. You see that the interior is dark. The doors are locked. Bill's Hardware is closed for business.

How can this be? A thousand thoughts run through your mind. What happened? What is Bill doing now? What happened to his staff? Did his business really close? Why? Was it a lack of sales? Was it ineffective advertising? Was it the wrong location? What's going to happen to Sparky?

When you calm down and begin to think, some reasons come to mind. Lately Bill was offering "free this and lowest price guaranteed that" specials. His bins and shelves were scattered and disorganized, making it hard to do your own sifting when Bill was preoccupied. There was just never enough of Bill to go around, whether or not his staff was there to help.

You liked Bill. He was a real guy who you felt cared about you. You would have gladly paid more if it meant keeping him in business. He always helped you find the right solution, whether it was digging through the bolt bins, ordering special parts or taking the time to explain benefits of a particular wire over another. Then something clicked and you thought of all those times he sold you something at lower than rock bottom prices. You remembered thinking "Did he make a mistake and mis-read the catalog price?" While your wallet was happy, you would wonder, "Shouldn't I be paying more? But I better not say anything, or he might change the price." Sadly, as nice as Bill was, he just under-performed and underpriced himself right out of business.

It's a shame, but this happens all too often. Nobody wins in this scenario. Not Bill, not his employees and not his customers. Even his landlord pays the price for Bill's mistake as now he has a space to lease. The rate at which businesses fail is alarming. I've chosen not to include actual statistics here as the numbers are so staggering it would put you in a very un-Zen tizzy and I need your best Zen Pillar of Focus moving forward. Now to address the elephant in the room - if you don't start thinking about customer experience and sustainable growth, you may find yourself sitting next to, you guessed it, Bill and his dog Sparky.

You've taken the road less travelled, created, and are now engaged in, what few people will ever experience - a business enterprise. I congratulate you. You're doing what many only dream about. I'm excited that you've picked up this book and allowed me to be a part of your creation. I'm honored and devoted to helping you continue your progress. Sometimes, that means serving you some cold hard facts. While starting an enterprise may be a bold move on your part and worthy of praise, that effort alone will not ensure that you are on the track to success.

There is, in fact, one very important aspect of being on the Zen Side of Business Ownership that you cannot take lightly. I'm talking about growing your business. You must understand and embrace the exchange cycles if you are to create an organization that will thrive beyond the next year and the decades that follow. You have an obligation to make your mark on the planet with your value proposition. Imagine all the staff and their families that you will support, all the customer promises you will fulfill, all the machinery you will buy, all the new offices you will decorate in your own Zen Patterns.

I get excited just thinking about how many of you will be great contributors to this economic market with your new Zen business. But you must ensure that there is a strong vision your customers can get behind and the financial wherewithal to make it further than next month. On the other side of the staggering statistics that reflect failed businesses, is the paradigm shift you can create for your business with a Zen mindset. You can blaze a new path of success inspiring other business owners to follow suit. You can change the perception of what business ownership can be. Most importantly, you can accomplish your goal to build an enterprise that is truly profitable - Zen Element #2. You can do this with a little bit of dreaming.

MOVEMENT 10: YOUR ZEN DREAM

So with our lead-in story in mind, let's contemplate a million-dollar question. What business are you in? I'm hearing you say something like "I'm in the business of helping people." Good, but wrong. "I'm in the business of making cool stuff." Wrong. "I'm in the business of creating." Wrong. "I'm in the business of making music."

Wrong. That is a lot of wrongs. So, what is the million-dollar answer? I'll give you one more chance and I'm counting on you to show me the light. "I'm in the business of revolutionizing my industry and making a mark on this planet with my Zenersity? Sorry, wrong again.

While I'm glad you remembered to leverage Your Zenersity in the last answer, you have much to absorb in this next section. Let me share the right answer in a subtle Zen tone. You are in the moneymaking business. Repeat – you need to make money. Pause for dramatic effect. You are not in the business of trading dollars. You are not in the business of helping people by selling things at cost. You are not in the business of bringing home a few extra dollars every week and living paycheck to paycheck. Be honest, no one starts a business without the goal of making money.

Conversely, you are in the business of purchasing new assets with the profits of your company that helps people. You are in the business of growing your staff. You are in the business of buying a bigger building that supports the creative world. Ideally, you are in the business of giving allocated money away to charities. You're turning a profit from day one and it's important that you do. Remember the early example of having a smaller car in which everything works? Well, pricing yourself for growth is one of the most integral elements to the whole equation of the Zen Side of Business Ownership. It's akin to the fuel in the car. The engine can now power the wheels, charge the air conditioner and all the electrical to get you moving down the road comfortably. Consider money as the very element that makes getting to your destination even possible. All the components depend on its flow and availability. Would you like to be driving the long haul and not even have enough battery to power the electricity to roll up the windows? Or worse, run out of fuel in the middle of nowhere?

You need cash and lots of it. That's more than likely why you started a business in the first place. You will need capital to buy tools for your trade. If you're pricing yourself to survive growth you can do it. You might argue that you are making money, but it's all tied up in projects. While this may appear to be a cash flow issue, it should be apparent that you don't have the resources to maintain growth and reinvest into other projects. So you might consider a loan. While there's nothing wrong with securing capital for growth, there's something about lending institutions, they tend to only lend to companies that make money. Would you loan money to a business without a solid way of making money? Banks and lenders are in the moneymaking business too. I keep driving this home because so many small businesses fail. This is the chapter where you need to shed your nice guy image.

Don't feel guilty for charging fair amounts of money for your product. Stop competing on price if you don't have the financial wherewithal to sustain it. If you're reading this and own a business, the statistics say that you won't be owning it for long. Why is this? While there are too many reasons to list here, the majority fail because they don't have enough operating capital to continue. Obviously, there are other reasons such as partnerships not working out, weather-related incidents, the lot. But Fortune 500 companies got to be where they are because they are profitable in a massive way and they continue to reinvest portions of that profit into their company for growth.

Consider the stock market. What kind of companies do potential shareholders seek out? They choose companies that are making money and anticipate future growth. It is easy to see in other businesses, yet in our own we feel that thriving is detrimental to the customer. It is un-Zen to provide an unworthy product or service for an overinflated price. But it's equally un-Zen to fall short of your potential and not charge that which will sustain growth. At this stage, you might be thinking that you charge good money for your products. Tell me though what your targeted profitability is for the year and what assets you intend to buy with it, by what date, and how it will secure growth for the remainder of the year. It is important to learn some basics about profitability, growth, and the expansions ahead. It all starts with making sure you're making money.

If you're having trouble with the concept of charging top dollar, and you still feel like it's not about the money, its time to reconsider your position. The world has trained all of us to think that charging too much for something is unethical and a practice that only the lowest of the lows employs. Of course, there are many other more important things in life than money. This chapter is not titled *"Rip Off Your Customer,"* it is appropriately titled *"Building Strong Roots."* You want to be around for a long time so you can continue to service your early faithful patrons as well as referrals and new customers.

I can't resist the opportunity to take a quick aside here. If money is rolling in without any end in sight and you really didn't care about it, then just think of what you could do with those dollars. Imagine how many charities you could help? What about Olympic athletes? I have a particular soft spot for Olympic athletes, people with remarkable amounts of talent, but not necessarily a lot of money, which they need to compete. So what about all that extra you've made. It can be put to good use and we can send our Olympians to the games with top-notch equipment and perhaps they can eat something more substantial than village cafeteria food. *(See link to donate in the appendix.)*

Now back to your plans for all those extra dollars. Realistically, since you're in the early stages of business and you are probably just thinking about affording your own meals without me suggesting you buy gourmet dishes for athletes you don't even know. But that's just it. You need to always be thinking about growth on a larger scale. Is this pricing idea starting to take shape for you? Need an example of what this looks like in the real world of consumerism? Let's consider the Concept Car.

Every year the world's major car builders assemble in Geneva, Frankfurt, Detroit and many other cities for the biggest display of concept cars found on the planet. These state-of-the-art car builds have one purpose - to demonstrate where the manufacturer hopes to be in five to ten years. These cars are not for sale and some don't even run properly. Most will never touch a street. But it doesn't matter. The point is to get the public to have a solid grasp of the future and what to expect from each carmaker. It's a way to gauge consumer enthusiasm, spot issues with potential buyers, and even serve as marketing power to stay at the top of web folds.

Development is great, but it comes at a cost. Some manufacturers spend more on research and development than others. But who really pays for the Concept Car? The manufacturer? No. The right answer is - you do. When you buy a car, sign the paperwork, and hand your money over to the dealership, a portion of that sale will fuel the "blue-sky" and future concept department. This constant stream of funding ensures that the manufacturer has a future for their cars, a direction, something to work towards. But here's the thing, automakers are no different than your business. Everyone has to adapt to new market needs, competition, and create new inventions that make their brand stand out. All Fortune 500 companies have campaigns. There's a new product release every month it seems and the funds to pay for the development of these new products comes from the product sales themselves. They are pricing to survive growth. Now it's your turn.

Implementing a blue sky concept department this early on might feel a little like putting the cart before the horse. I can't stress enough that you must make growth costs a part of your budget and subsequent product pricing from the beginning. Perhaps you are in the formative years of business ownership and you are charging only what will keep you afloat. Maybe you're still learning your craft and working out all the kinks. But remember this, every cost you'll ever have is going to increase. This is a fact of business ownership. Trade regulations, technology developments, market changes, inflation, all are and will continue to be a part of your world in some capacity.

As you move through the business ranks, understanding and embracing these dynamic components will serve you well because there is no fulfillment in stagnation. You started a business because you were seeking the opposite of mundane. Your business is a conglomeration of ever-changing elements that you cleverly maneuver into profitable configurations. The moment you develop momentum with one layout, one of these components will likely change, thus creating a new set of challenges. This is all part of the cycle. Insurance, fuel, minimum wage, bank fees, these are ever-changing contributors to the larger entity you call your business, that which depends on the resources made available to you. This is a good thing. You need them to thrive to expand their services which will, in turn, help expand your services. Let's remember what this chapter is all about - strong roots. The buck stops with you. You must stay far ahead of these changes. Anticipate them. Plan for them. Price for them. This is your ticket to a long career on the Zen Side of Business Ownership.

You are now going to plan like the "big boys." This means making a concerted effort to rearrange the way you price yourself. To that end, clearly defining what your "product" really is just might be the key to tie these hypotheticals together for you. In the spirit of this book, a small change of perspective will reveal what your deliverable really is: particularly, one word that may have escaped your line of sight. What is this magic word? It starts with the letter "D."

Up until now you might have perceived your end product to be the delivery or moment of exchange of your tangible item or service. That's what you've been "pricing." It seems logical, right? The thing you hand to your customers as you say thank you. The product or service that you've worked so hard to create while meeting face to face with your customer delivering the line, "I hope you really enjoyed your experience. And please come back again."

Isn't that our perception, whether we view the exchange through the eyes of the business owner, patron, or broader consumer? But is this the definition that serves your business best? You see your creation and currency make the exchange and, from a business owner's perspective, you might think, "Yes! I just doubled my money by selling this widget!" That might be hitting it out of the ballpark or it may be way below the bar. As we've learned from our plant kingdom example and corresponding Zenersity in Chapter One, every business is different. Doubling capital might be sufficient for certain types of business transactions and fall short for others. The underlying question and bigger issue that needs addressing is this: Per your business, are you pricing for the larger growth scene at hand? Perhaps. Well, I now present the word that will make all the difference for you – the one that starts with a D - dream.

If ever there was a Zen Movement that rivals Your Zen Offering, Your Zen Dream is it. In the seemingly rigid black and white pricing world of service delivery, this grayishly soft, underestimated, underutilized term is your salvation. This is the thing that moves your business into the direction you've envisioned.

Consider this as comparable to mapping out all the stops you need to make in the car trip we experienced together early on in the Preface of this book. You now know all the service stations to refuel, where you plan to eat, the places you'll pull over to take a few selfies and the anticipated costs along the way. The journey just got real. It's tangible. This will now be the standard by which you operate. Not only that, this is the perspective from which your customer will operate.

Now for another set of questions. How will Your Zen Dream become apparent to your customer and why will they care? How will they buy into the idea of your dream? How can you expect your customers to make a shift from simply purchasing the commodity or service you offer to something as obscure as a dream? Can you even "sell" a dream? You can and here's how. Reevaluate your price point to include growth costs and educate your customers along every step of the way. Make sure they know how their support is advancing the business, right down to the new machine you want to purchase or the storefront with improved parking. This dream can get awfully expensive. So your asking price will most likely be above a perceived market yield. This does not mean the end of your business or stream of patrons. On the contrary, it means the beginning of your growth.

Is this making sense? Your Zen Dream is the differentiator and you are selling it. Your future expansions and plans must be very tangible for both you and your patrons. Every sale you make gets you one step closer to buying that new machine or hiring for that long-awaited new staff member. You are not just "getting by." You are growing. From now on, when you make the sale, you are meeting face to face with your customer delivering the line. "I hope you really enjoyed your experience with us. Please look over this brochure showing future plans to improve our service commitments and products. I hope you will make the journey with us and continue to support our mission."

There's a difference with the above approach. Something interesting happens when your customer is included in the future vision of your company. They begin to take you more seriously. You will stand out as the achiever you are and begin to create the momentum you need. Every time you hear the cash register ring, you will smile knowing that your "trip" is being funded and you're on your way. It's in our human nature to get behind causes in which we believe.

Speaking of those causes, isn't that why many of us support Olympic hopefuls. We hear the stories of endless training and overcoming setbacks. These are the passions that make life worth living. Supporting those who strive to achieve the seemingly impossible makes us feel part of something special. Events such as these are captivating. For one minute we can watch one person or a team, who have trained incessantly to do one thing - be the best in the world. The inspiration is contagious. What precedes these star athletes' performance parallels your new modus operandi. That close-up interview where athletes spell out their visions, ambitions, and goals associated with the successes they hope to achieve – their dream.

You are no different. You have a dream for your company and your customer needs to know what it is. Your Zen Dream! The super image you hold in your mind's eye; the future you who has new, bigger, faster machines. The you with triple the staff. The you who no longer simply operates day to day and is working on future developments. The you who will make their experience better. That is what your customer is purchasing and that is what you are pricing.

That million-dollar question now comes full circle. Does your customer know of Your Zen Dream and do they know what their contribution is making possible for you, for your growth, and ultimately for them? Most likely they do not, so it's time for action. Chapter One is about to make its comeback. Remember Your Zen Offering? You will now be strengthening that beautiful offering you've created. Take out your exercise sheet from Chapter One and place it directly before you.

Exercise 6A

It's Zen Dream time. Write down everything you need to make your future offering a reality. These essentials will put you in the best possible position to deliver a bigger, better version of Your Zen Offering this year, next year, and in five years. How many staff members will you need? How many do you need now? How much square footage office space is optimal? How many locations do you hope to open and by when?

What will it take to produce the best offering? Dreaming big is not discouraged in this exercise. Just as there is no harm in deciding how far you want to make your hypothetical trip, there is no limit as to how far you stretch your list of attainable assets. It is important that you draw out your road map in detail. Make clear distinctions between short-term and long-term purchases. Develop something you can hold in front of your customer and say, "We will be adding this widget to our facility next year to further improve your experience." The more time you spend listing out all the improvements you would like to see, the more excitement and passion you begin to generate towards that growth. The places that you will stop, the amount of fuel it will take and so on and so forth.

Maybe you want the most expensive machine money can buy. But is there a machine that will get the job done and help you work your way to the top of the line model? That's what you want, clear steps leading to an ambitious destination. The clearer you are about those milestones, the easier it will be to gauge if your current pricing is in alignment with your future purchases. Perhaps you have some adjusting to do. Small goals are equally encouraged. Perhaps you would like to buy new folders for the company. Maybe you'd like to have some stickers made to brand your business. It's all on the table. Every time you check a Zen Dream item off the list, you will be making the very progress you've been inadvertently stifling by selling things too close to cost. This is no small victory. You have a future to work toward and a pricing strategy that will get you there. But you're not out of the woods yet. Your next objective is to move your customer from their state of ignorance to reciting every Zen Dream line item you've created right back to you. They need to know it all and you need to figure out how this happens.

Exercise 6B

Write down a goal enlightenment strategy for your customer. How will they learn of your new goals list? The creativity is completely up to you. Is it a newsletter that goes out or a pamphlet that you hand deliver? Is it a brochure that goes into every package you sell? A phone call? An email? Find whatever it takes to get your message heard. If your newsletter goes straight to your customer's trash folder then you haven't pushed your creativity far enough. It is imperative that your customer learns of your goals and hears the progress reports. What have you checked off your list? What is the next purchase going to be? How many more staff have you hired because of their continued support.

Give your customers a reason to get behind you. Let them know that with every dime they spend, it means one more step closer to a better experience for them. You determine the method and high marks are awarded for the most effective. When you accomplish this, it will spark the beginning of your growth. Your company will stand out. Your customers will begin to perceive you differently. You will resonate as the service provider who means business, a business that's serious about growth. Really? How will they know? With all this dreaming and a higher entry price point, your customer is going to be waiting for the best song and dance they've ever seen. Because when you charge for the dream, you must be ready to deliver it. It's time to bring on Your Zen Phenomenon.

MOVEMENT 11: YOUR ZEN PHENOMENON

You've made your case known. Your customer knows what you're all about and they're tingling with anticipation. So now what? You have a slew of anxious patrons who are giving your new ideas a go by jumping on board Your Zen Dream. They are now entitled to sit back and see if you are who you say you are. Are you prepared for the work that lies ahead? It's showtime.

If you are the future visionary in your industry with the new gadgets coming as you claim, then all should be well, right? Your customer has paid the new entrance price and they're sitting restlessly in the bleachers waiting to see a performance that will knock their socks off. What you whip up next is completely on you. The ball is in your court. Will you "ooh" and "aah" them with Your Zen Offering? The stakes just got higher and there's a lot to deliver. There's a crescendo of tension as the spotlight singles you out. The curtains are opening. You have a chance to prove your worth and move one step closer to your new asset. Queue the music.

I have to interject. The show's about to start and I need to make sure we're on the same page moving forward. Time to take a step back and look at our old friend Bill the hardware store owner. Is there a thing or two we can learn from the story to help us with our performance? Remember Bill, the one who held an ever-knowledgeable collection of solutions to your weekend headaches? You liked him. But there was something missing. You weren't entirely sold on the whole experience. As much as you liked Bill, you struggled with the wait time as he helped other customers with meticulous detail. On top of that, his shop was just this side of disorganized so you couldn't even help yourself. But you couldn't blame him. He was just one guy with a couple of helpers and Sparky trying to handle the world's problems. You were third or fourth in line for Bill's attention.

That just wasn't good enough to win you over. So, could there have been a way for you to get what you needed and still keep him in business? A way that you could have reaped the benefits of his expertise without having to wait a lifetime? Even if it meant paying a wee bit more? Yes, absolutely! You just need the tool that will make all the difference, a light that will have your customers standing in full jaw-dropping amazement. Imagine this; what if Bill was there just waiting for you to swing into the door ready to hear your troubles? How would that experience make you feel? Knowing that everything would be okay. Lucky for you, that alternate timeline does exist and it's achievable with what's to follow. It's time to define one of your most powerful movements - Your Zen Phenomenon.

You've got a big task ahead of you! Your mission is to knock your audience dead – figuratively (this *is* a Zen book after all). But let's not forget, your company's reputation is on the line. One slip up and......oh dear. That's not going to happen. You are going to rock it. You are going to create an experience like no other.

You are going to hit it out of the ballpark. Any baseball fans here? For those who have ever played for fun or watched a game, it won't be hard to call forth the euphoria associated with a Grand Slam. It brings the sound of a momentous crack of the bat against the ball launching it into the stratosphere by your team hero. It's a reverberation felt throughout the stadium, a moment that can change the outcome of the game in an instant. In this emotionally charged event, there's a point in time that is truly magical; a nano-second where you experience a transformation, when time stops.

Sure, there's intensity when the pitch is released. A shock when the ball is crushed. But there's an even more piercing experience that happens just after these key points. There's no feeling like the second you realize the ball isn't coming back. It's gone. That's when those butterflies in your stomach start to flutter. Yes. That's the moment I'm referring to. That's Your Zen Phenomenon - the moment you will now be creating.

With a little Zen magic, Bill could have won you over. If he had had the financial wherewithal to afford full time staffing assigned to organization, inventory, ordering, point of sales, and additional customer service advisors, things would have been very different. Imagine when you went to Bill's store he welcomes you into a meeting room with a chalkboard waiting to go over your project. A staff member then takes on the remainder of the job and pulls parts from the shelf for you. Yet another rings you up and arranges a follow up. Bill's team is onsite and ready to handle your problems with the snap of a finger. You're in and out with a solid plan of action. But it wouldn't stop there; one of Bill's trained advisors calls you back to ensure things are going according to plan, to thank you for the business and make sure that all is well.

Do you see the difference? That sort of experience would leave you speechless. Imagine the customer reviews. You would surely find yourself talking to others about the experience. Of course it would cost more for Bill to do business this way. The work of creating the space, designing the Zen patterning and the time needed to perfect the formula. This is not a modest undertaking. But if there's one thing you've learned in your experience as a business owner, it's that time is money. Bill just found a way to keep the job he loved most by being the first point of contact and still raise his customers' experience to new heights, as in stratospheric levels. Feel the butterflies stirring?

You are now charged with the momentous responsibility of creating an emotional imprint of that scale from here on. What is Your Zen Phenomenon? It is the experience you deliberately create in perfect sequence for your customer. This is the measuring stick by which you will be judged. It's the impression you make. It is your calculated rollout of steps that lead your patron to realize what you're all about. You are the magician who pulls a rabbit out of your hat while everyone stands back in disbelief saying, "How did you do that?"

You've masterfully created Your Zen Offering, sold your customer on Your Zen Dream, and now you'll bring them to their knees with a perfect execution of your service. It doesn't matter if you are a "one man show" or a company of 1000. Create Your Zen Phenomenon with whatever resources you have available to you. You must over-deliver. It is imperative that you achieve an 11 out of 10 scoring from your customer's perspective, not yours. Did you get that? Your customer has to originate the sentiment. It's equivalent to your Grand Slam sending the ball past the stadium walls and smashing the very windshield of the car you drove in on.

Repair costs aside, isn't that a story worth telling your friends, all the while, clutching the very baseball that broke your glass? Wouldn't that make your batting hero a legend in your books forever? Yes, that moment, my Zen protégés, is what you are striving for. Your definitive goal is to leave a lasting impression on your customer. Like the magician, you'll tell your audience first how you will dazzle them; the magic up your sleeve they will soon experience born from your offering using all your Zen Movements. Then, execute the final bang, one that will have them sit back in their chair and say, "Wow, I'll never go anywhere else." Or, "I've never seen anyone deliver like this." That's your target aim. You will absolutely gauge success by the response of your customer at the very least, as a sentiment or compliment that always follows your performance.

If you really want to create a customer for life and solidify growth, you have to slam the ball straight out of the park and break their windshield, evoking utter disbelieve, awe, and maybe even an expletive! You want to hear a few choice words. That's when you know you've hit it. Your delivery needs to be unparalleled by all standards. This relentless striving for the perfect experience is what your promise and exchange of currency is all about. You've made the commitment to have an experience with a new customer and now you will deliver that plus much, much more. You have the tool that will ensure the scales tip in your favor for long-term growth, the action that will create a customer for life. Mastering Your Zen Phenomenon is the final action that will ensure the creation of strong growth roots forever!

Now it's exercise time. You have the Zen Movements to put you on the podium and the metric by which to gauge yourself. So the question now is, what is your personal Zen Phenomenon?

Exercise 6C

You're assignment is to take a step back and write out your measuring tool, the thing your customer will say or do after they've experienced your offering. What is it going to be? It can be an action such as evoking a customer to immediately post about your product. It can simply be hearing the phrase, "Thank you for going far beyond the call of duty. I'll be back soon." Or perhaps it's, "No one has ever passed all four QC checks on the first try." You've worked so hard to make the sale. Beyond the exchange of currency, what do you most want your customer to do that will ensure future growth, whether it's through continued business or spreading the word? Imagine if your customers were so dazzled, they returned with another smiling face while shouting the line, "See this place, I told you you'd be blown away."

The more relevant and ambitious your measuring stick is, the greater the financial impact. You're not measuring the cash entering the register, per se, you are creating your indicators. A realization of those indicators in turn ensures cash in the register. You can instantly see a prosperous future on the fast track to growth. Just like Your Zen Offering, no two answers will be the same. Create Your Zen Phenomenon as your own. So, what's it going to be? Imagine what sort of diverse world of future business experiences awaits you from this exploration.

Chapter Take Aways

Your Zen Dream is what its all about as you secure your current business efforts and plan for future growth. What do you need to make this dream happen, how can you price your products to make that dream a reality now and for years to come. It's time to create your list of future assets for your customers, your employees and your company so together, with the support of all three, Your Zen Dream won't fade from lack of financial resources.

Your Zen Phenomenon; Finding that one thing that brings on the butterflies of excitement is Your Zen Phenomenon. Discover how you can over deliver to your customer with that "wow" that will bring them back and make them your biggest promoters.

PERFECT YOUR OFFERING

AND MORE IMPORTANTLY, PERFECT YOUR CUSTOMER!

W elcome to All Flavors, your place for home-town family froZen fun! How may I help you?

To start this chapter, imagine yourself in a far-off land of froZen treats and icy fun. It's time to take a break and live vicariously through a hypothetical case study. All Flavors is your family legacy ice creamery. It's every bit a mom and pop operation and known throughout the land for its famous homemade French Vanilla. This business has afforded your family a living for over a century, supporting generations. Its future is now in your lap. It's you, watching the day to day; you who shows up to put smiles on children's faces. Serving the community and making a profit all the while - the earmarks of a Zen business. So, time to toast to your success? After all, you were born into the craft in early childhood, making you nothing short of a French Vanilla guru as an adult.

You love your rich culture through and through. In fact,

you know virtually everything there is to know on the subject with years of finessing recipes to perfection. So naturally, in your parlor, your guests are afforded the opportunity to taste the experience of your handmade legacy – that rich and creamy absolutely delectable French Vanilla. This is your family's secret recipe that you make from scratch to utter perfection. But, as you try to keep business booming, you find that your creation of french purism and originality is contrasted by something you are less passionate about - other flavors.

In an effort to hedge your French home run and offer more, you now stock an array of mediocre alternatives from a wholesaler down the way. Cookies 'n Cream, Chocolate Chip, Rainbow, Mint, even Bubble Gum - all poor substitutes to your French creation but making your All Flavors name true. Despite this ridiculously massive oversight, I mean, minor detail, you face the market armed with an arsenal of flavors under one roof. You're ready to serve as the conduit between a warm body and a widely diversified froZen inventory. As a result, your company is just this side of profitable generating cash flow in the hot seasons and sustaining itself through the slow ones. There is a lot to be proud of with your business. You draw a decent salary, can take time off when you like and are able to employ local help.

Your staff knows how to scoop the ice cream just the right way to make the customers happy and not drain the inventory too fast. They memorized your tagline. "Welcome to All Flavors, your place for home-town family froZen fun," the magical line that welcomes each customer. Pitching the family component to remind folks this business is not a chain. Everything is great, except, as no story is complete without an arch nemesis, enter in the hypothetical Bob's Creamery, just down the way. Bob's has a bit more financial backing and structure. There's always a consistent stream of patrons coming in and out. Bob's Creamery has even more flavors, more parking spaces, more cones, more machines and more seats. Bob's has more of everything. Frankly its very irritating and doesn't help your bottom line.

You have some business to take care of, you have to take down Bob's and fast. Your chosen weapon of attack - All Flavors' Wednesday Special. On Wednesdays, you hang a massive banner outside that reads, "Half-Off Today!" Inside, your generic walls painted in dull pastel colors, boast posters of the popular flavors and ads that read, "Buy Two - Get One Free!". There's a beautiful hand painted sign to point out family famous French Vanilla which gets lost among all this hodgepodge.

When someone actually reads that sign and asks about this special flavor, you really get passionate. You come alive telling them about how the whole idea was born in France decades ago. You can talk about the history all day long. But unfortunately, each experience is short lived. Most who inquire just hassle you for free tastes. They aren't prepared (or could care less) to hear your life's story. In fact most of the warm bodies are just patrons who would rather have a scoop of the generic stuff you don't even make; taking bites of the mass-produced magic, making satisfactory expressions and remarking something to the tune of, "It's good, Thanks." Frustrating.

Despite this travesty, all this Un-Zen is overshadowed by a fleeting moment of bliss when somebody actually buys your special French Vanilla. The family legacy resonates. You are fulfilled. It's obvious, your real passion isn't entirely All Flavors-driven, its sharing your family's French Vanilla that takes your breath away. In spite of all this, you show up every day hoping things will be different. Just maybe you'll fall in love with the creamery once again. Because on the one hand, you love having a business, ice-cream is what you know, and you're passionate about your family legacy. But on the other, you don't care about all those other flavors made by someone else.

But down the way you can see that Bob's Creamery does care. You've heard the tales of founder Bob waking up at 2 a.m. with a magical recipe for Cookies n' Cream, followed by Mint Chip and other flavors too crazy to mention. They are going gangbusters, lines out the door every day. So then it must follow, if you're going to call yourself an ice-cream shop, you better start dreaming about all the flavors. If you don't, how can you expect to take over the ice-cream market share in your area? But you don't even like Cookies n' Cream.

Consider the hard facts for a moment. On one hand, French Vanilla embodies your family and you are well aware of what the ice cream making business has done for your ancestors. But on the other hand, Bob's is light years ahead of you in operating a successful business. Are trade-offs just a part of business? Are you forever doomed to a life of false pretense? Does this insurmountable conundrum ever end? Yes it can. With a little sprinkle of Zen, you can turn this around and make operating your business fulfilling again. It is possible to have your ice-cream and eat it too; serving the right ice cream and the right customers. You are about to discover the importance of honing in your offering and hand selecting the perfect customers. If you don't dial-in this all too important element, you'll never truly hit the target of serving a community of people - Zen Element #4. So here to help you do that is the next Zen Movement, Your Zen Pairing.

MOVEMENT 12: YOUR ZEN PAIRING

Let's get back to our ice cream store example. You may have a good thing going with All-Flavors, but it's not great. It's not wow! You are not operating on the Zen Side of Business Ownership. You're doing what most business owners typically do. You are adjusting your offering to match your competitors. As a result, Your Zen Phenomenon has now dwindled down to nothing. Your customers' all too frequent comments like, "It's good, thanks," hurt. The mediocrity is hard to stomach. You want to hear, "This is nothing like I've ever tasted before, it's delicious." As much as you'd like to blame this lack of enthusiasm on the idea that Bob's dictates your business decisions, there's a little more going on than meets the eye.

Look closer. Even if you had the magic button to make Bob's Creamery vanish, you would still struggle. Why is this? On top of the multitude of flavors, I mean, reasons, it's obvious that Your Zen Offering needs fine tuning. Being the avid Zen protege you've become, you can spot the lack of Zenersity in our opener. You are selling something that does not truly embody you. If you've really been paying attention, you would place that "red flag" right into Bin #1 from Chapter 4 to be reconciled, fast.

You have diluted Your Zen Offering into a hodgepodge of what could best be described as compromise. You offer an arsenal of flavors and don't care about most of them. But still, every day you hope the multitude of customers entering your creamery will look past the glass case of colorful ice cream bins to the hand painted sign and ask for a bite of your family's famous French Vanilla. You find yourself agonizing while watching customers point to the Cookies 'n Cream or Mint Chip, or anything other than French Vanilla and then remarking, "It's good, thanks." Not "great," not "wow," not, "I'll take another one please." Unfortunately, you set yourself up for these mediocre responses. And to what end? Just to beat Bob's Creamery at his own, well-planned game?

As business owners, we've been trained to diversify ourselves right out of the community of people we could best serve. We seek to defend and protect our business by capturing every warm body within a hundred-mile radius. By doing so, something detrimental happens.

As the owner of our hypothetical creamery, ask yourself this - is the person standing on the other side of the counter the right one for you? Before you answer, consider these points. You offer plenty of ice cream. It's right there in the case. But before you push the sale, do you truly believe that customer standing in front of you will suddenly jump for joy over your diluted offering when hundreds before did not? If you're like a number of business owners in the marketplace, you'll brush past this paramount detail and continue to push the sale until you hear the words, "I'll take it!" Guess what? You know how this ends. Naturally your customer will pay you, take a bite, make a weird expression, and perpetuate the cycle you dread every day. "It's good, thanks."

It's time to stop spinning your Zen wheels with customers who are not a good fit. All too often, we as eager business seekers presume that we can change our customers' perspective. But it's time you learned a hard lesson - it's not your job to change people. It's not your job to convince everyone on the planet that you are the best.

To put it plainly, you have the right to like the things you do. Other people have the right to like the things they do. It is not your job to change people. This chapter is titled "Perfect your offering and your customer," not "What if you could change all the people around you to like your product?" So think again. Is ensuring that everyone within a hundred-mile radius interacts with your offering a winning strategy? Of course, a new sale presents a chance to convince a patron that All-Flavors is a better proposition than another alternative. You are always encouraged to have lofty Zen Phenomena that aim to change the world. This segment is about honing in your offering and making sure you have the right customer in front of you. You want customers who are promoters, believers in your business. You want people who are worthy of Your Zen Pounce so you never ever hear those unenthusiastic words. "It's good, thanks."

Building your business around the notion of changing people is going to lead to a lot of customer turnover and a very un-Zen state. Regardless of any excitement over your offering, as well as the innovative creation you stand for, you will always fall short of Your Zen Phenomenon if you don't have the right person standing on the other side of the register. You must first understand something about the person who just walked in your door. People are perfectly happy with the buying solutions they have been accustomed to, as they should be. This is a planet of choice when it comes to consumerism, for good reason. We are diverse beings with our own unique stories and preferences. This uniqueness is interwoven into our person and is part of us right down to the food we eat, the clothes we wear, the places that make us feel good, etc. Your business model is not about taking over market share you have no Zenersity to infuse it with. It's about being the best you, searching for the right customer to bring into your circle. The world has a special place just for you, so fill it by selecting the customers that match you. Welcome in Your Zen Pairing.

Picture yourself in a warehouse full of green socks. There is a maze of towering bins of emerald colored socks, an endless sea of monotonously arranged textiles. There you are, smack dab in the middle with a golden sock in your possession. You are now tasked with the responsibility of finding the other cleverly hidden glorious match - your golden pair. You have five minutes to make this a reality. You have one vibrant glimmering sock and it's imperative that you find the magical bin containing its companion somewhere in the maze.

You're looking for anything in this massive complex that can get you to Golden Sock Avenue, fast. How do you do it? It all depends on your ability to look down a given aisle, scan vigorously, and quickly move toward the next promising pile. Do you see a clear parallel to your new modus operandi on customer selection? You will stop the cycle of pretending that green looks close enough to call it golden. You will ignore the bins of green socks in front of you and move on to other more promising bins. In your business, customer selection is much the same as this sock hunt. Sifting quickly past the wrong customers to identify and embrace the right ones.

There is an entire group of people who would rush to be first in line to try your product and who are equally passionate about learning more about Your Zen Offering. What a shame it would be if, by broadening your offering to match every competitor, you miss providing service to those who would benefit the most from knowing you. Is it so bad to lose a customer to a competitor if it wasn't someone who was right for your business? It's time to stop this competitive insanity. You must, at all costs, be very selective about who makes their way into your parlor.

If you let the wrong person in, you keep the right person out, plain and simple. So who should you let pass through your doors? Your mission is to ensure you discern the right candidates from the wrong ones. It can be tricky, very tricky. Because while many people might like sweets, or pie, and even ice-cream, there's only a select few who love the same thing you do, for instance, homemade French Vanilla.

To put this in perspective, picture a movie box office release and the potential patrons who'd pay to see it. There are people who like to go to movies, right? On the other side of the spectrum, there are sci-fi enthusiasts. This special breed of folks is willing to camp out for days on end, in costume, to watch the next release. Technically, both the regular moviegoer and the sci-fi enthusiast could be lumped into a movie customer category. But can you really support such an argument? One patron has the product in their DNA and eats, sleeps and breathes spaceships. The other person just likes the occasional new movie. Imagine a scenario in which the movie theater only had one seat for the release of your new sci-fi film. Which customer would you, the director of the film, hope would be chosen to watch it and review it? You guessed it - the guy wearing the alien costume, of course. It's so easy to see. Yet we as business owners spend most of our time trying to convince the regular movie patron that our sci-fi movie is the best, and they respectively give us the blank stare and say, "It's good, thanks."

In the early stages of your business, you have a limited capacity to service customers. If you're tied up with the lukewarm moviegoer, you probably keep the sci-fi fanatic out. The one guy who was going to talk up the movie to all his buddies and recommend your film to more of his costume-wearing friends. That's what you want, more of that guy. Why do we still accept the line "I like movies", when what we really want to hear is: "I love green aliens that attack the hero with a Z-21 spacecraft. I once camped for three days waiting for the release of the –"

Think you don't have the luxury of vetting? That your doors must be open to everyone, and you have to serve them all? The answer is a no; you can hand pick your customers. Always. Of course, you must maintain a professional operation at all times. But don't forget, your business is on the line. This lesson has nothing to do with shoving somebody out of your business and everything to do with scanning your market and clearly knowing which customers are going to skyrocket you into the next financial tier.

Everyone worries over that customer who marches down the street to the competition because what you have doesn't excite. In actuality this is exactly what you want. Nothing is worse than being in a relationship where one person isn't committed. Why would you put yourself through that? Birds of a feather flock together. You want the wrong bird to fly away to another shop and the right birds to come to yours.

Why is this customer distinction important? As the ever positive and eager businesspeople we are, it can be easy to imagine that all the green socks in the warehouse could be a match for the gold one you're holding. We see ourselves surrounded by crowds of people all wanting what we have to offer. But is this the makings of a symbiotic eternal Zen Pairing? Will any of the bustling green sock customers ever be a true match to your single golden sock? I believe in abundance in all respects. But we are not training you to be all things to all people. The universe has a special place just for you. So look at this challenge from a different perspective. While I support the position that you should never give up on reaching your unlimited potential and possibility, quality wins over quantity in the Zen world. We are looking for one particular type of sock in one particular color. This vigorous scan and selection is what Your Zen Pairing is all about. The end result will resemble a private party invitation more than a flash mob. In fact, for every one golden Zen Pairing you attain, you may have had to slip past 40 to 50 green ones. Be assured the extra effort is well worth it. For when you finally discover your hidden match, you've got a partner for life, a return customer, a true promoter of you and your business.

Your Zen Pairing experience should be predictable and controlled. It should feel like a warm intimate dinner where all your guests are seated and dressed for the occasion. An experience for which they have eagerly waited in anticipation for whatever beautiful concoction you're stirring up for them to enjoy. They'll be turning to you with excitement and awe as to how they could have found such a terrific provider, product, or service.

You might look back at them and wonder what you did to deserve their loyal patronage and enthusiasm. Interactions will be genuine and heart felt. There's a reciprocating appreciation for each other's position. You are now serving a community of people and being true to yourself. Do you like the thought of an intimate party with your close family of supporters? How much more Zen can you get? This is where you are headed. This is your new future. Before this section reaches its end you will have the recipe for the delicious soiree you've been craving since the inception of your business. It's time to start the process of identifying the match that will bring the spark back into your life. Prepare to reset your guiding compass and find your golden sock.

Exercise 7A

Phase 1 of Your Zen Pairing involves 1) you, 2) your notepad, and 3) a bit of soul searching. It's time to go on a sentimental journey. Take a deep breath and jump into the driver seat. We are going down nostalgia lane. Write down the top 10 fondest memories you've experienced while owning your own business or if you are contemplating starting a business, then reflect upon your field. Use the list below to help you resurrect those memories. Later, you'll break down the findings into the very things that will catapult your efforts. Ready? Write down all the moments in your business ownership history that made you:

1. Come alive with passion!
2. Appreciate having the best job in the world.
3. Strive hard to reach an accomplishment.
4. See yourself as "In Your Element."

To help you through this very important drill, here is an example using our hypothetical creamery.

Reflect:

Ice cream feels like home. It's comforting. The French Vanilla family recipe was something you held near and dear to your heart. You loved growing up on a farm, how your family made a living and how closely you all needed to work together to get things done. You loved the routines, the seasons you experienced while performing the functions of the job. You fondly remember how an icy dessert followed every meal and how you sometimes helped to improve it. You loved being a part of something bigger than you. You loved watching folks eat your special creations and thanking your family for the wonderful treat. Your customers depended on you to be there.

Create Your List:

Create a list of bullet points that organize the thoughts above.

French Vanilla
Family lineage
Ice-cream
Social contributions
Routines
Making a living from craft
Times of day (morning, afternoons or evenings)
Specialty recipes
Family Values
Seasons

In the years you've owned your business, have you ever taken a moment to write out all the things that make you come alive as you've done here? Have you assessed the real reasons you wake up each day to create your commerce? This all too important exercise is overshadowed with emergencies, fires, and concerns about your competitors: gauging success only by your ability to make payroll. Your passions are important. They are the key to your happiness and ultimately what define you. Congratulations on making it to Phase 2 of Your Zen Pairing exercise.

Exercise 7B

Rank your list of favorite moments from good to better to best. Write all three categories on a sheet and place your nostalgic moments in a ranking saving your best for last. How do you know you've done it correctly? Because when you start reading the list, you'll feel the excitement. With each passing point that energy should skyrocket until you find yourself tearing up. Okay maybe hold the tears, but, get as close as you can. For your creamery, this exercise might look like the following:

(Would be good to fit in three columns on a page or in a table.)

GOOD:
Ice-cream
Routines
Specialty recipes

BETTER:
Family Values
Times of day (morning, afternoons or evenings.)
Social Contributions

BEST:
French Vanilla
Seasons
Making a living from craft
Family lineage

Exercise 7C

Now take your list of points and twist them ever so slightly to make them reveal something special. In two stages add a few new words and Your Zen Pairing will glimmer like a ray of sunlight illuminating a priceless jewel.

7C.a) Add the word "Zen Pairings" after each of the header good; better; and best.

7C.b) Add the phrase "Customers who love" before each of your nostalgic moments from the previous list.

Your Creamery's Zen Pairing list is complete and might look like the following:

GOOD (Zen Pairings):
Customers who love ice cream
Customers who love routines
Customers who love specialty recipes

BETTER (Zen Pairings):
Customers who love Family Values
Customers who love times of day (morning, afternoons or evenings.)
Customers who love regional culture

BEST (Zen Pairings):
Customers who love French Vanilla
Customers who love seasons
Customers who love making a living from his/her craft
Customers who love family lineage

Congratulations! You've just discovered the row number and bin of your matching golden sock. Still wish you could beat Bob's Creamery at its own game? Hardly. You have way too much Zen standing in front of you to ignore. You now know who the person on the other side of the counter ought to be, someone from the Best Zen Pairing category. Someone who welcomes you with open arms and is worthy of Your Zen Pounce. Someone you can connect with and rescue easily. A lost soul who's been waiting to see what you've been cooking up - your sci-fi fanatic!

The absolute best customers for you are those who love French Vanilla, the seasons, appreciate those who make a living from their own craft, and those who love family lineage. Ensuring that it is these customers who stand before you manifests Zenergistic success, that magic that will catapult you into stardom. What of the remaining categories? Should you ignore them? Absolutely not. Everyone in the three groups would do well to enjoy the Creamery's new focus, specialty French Vanilla Ice Cream and a rich family culture. Now you have a much more tailored offering that embodies Your Zenersity.

Your creamery will be the best for delivering seasonal

French Vanilla flavors with a twist of family values, hands down. The category-pairing guide represents the right folks who will anxiously anticipate this whole new direction. This new guiding compass will initiate contact with these customers using different methods than before. Banners? Half-off specials? You're done with that. Outreach and connection is now a different and focused game.

You are crystal clear on just who makes the cut and is worthy of interacting with your product. You will now have adjusted Your Zen Focus straight at your top ten Zen Pairings. So instead of the old marketing routine, you spend your marketing time with laser focus on cooking magazines, travel agencies and local museums. Places where foreign exploration, winning recipes, and appreciation of culture are prominent. You're sure to advertise in family periodicals, certain do-it-yourself forums, and even websites focused on seasonal celebrations. All of these new areas represent a chance to employ Your Zen Tap with great success to a group of patrons already curious about your business.

The absolute highest version of your business is about to unfold before you. It takes both the right offering and the right customer to make magic happen. With all your training, you have the recipe to perfect both of these and bring it all together.

So what does your hypothetical creamery, operating on the Zen Side of Business Ownership, look like now?

The Finale - La Vie de Vanille.

Customers are greeted with a genuine "Bienvenue!" (Welcome) as they enter. You've employed French culture everywhere. The business name is "La Vie de Vanille" (The Vanilla Life). A beautiful new interior and experience represents Your Zen Offering better than ever, embodying every bit of you.

For your new Zen Offering.... *(C^Z = YZO)*

You are now the first in your industry to combine __ *(C) the home made craft of French Vanilla__* raised to new levels of ___ *(^{Z}) Family lineage, culture, geography, and seasons__* to create __ *(YZO) a "home grown" French countryside experience at varying times of the day, month, or year__* for your customers. Your Zen Offering redesigned and complete, check!

You've revamped the business from top to bottom. Your location now has a warm homey feeling with mocha colored walls featuring accents of distressed wood and vintage family photos sprinkled throughout. Old generic posters have been replaced with illustrated boards displaying your rich family history. The location embodies a beautiful country barn modeled after your great grandma's farm - the place it all started. Overhead is the family crest, a coat of arms celebrating your lineage. Your Zen Reflection, check!

The ambiance doesn't stop there. It is evident everywhere top to bottom right down to the berets your staff wears along with an accenting country farm apron embroidered with the matching family crest. Look, here comes someone now. No need to worry, this isn't just a lukewarm moviegoer. Not by far. How would you know? Well, before you can say "Bienvenue!", you're asked about the song playing throughout. The historical accordion piece over the stereo setting the mood. This reaction is your clue to who stands before you. So with that, you walk your new guest over to the backstory wall to begin your French family narrative. Your Zen Pairing, check!

Your renovated space is divided into quadrants with each wall prominently highlighting an aspect of the business including your family's ice cream-making history. It's a timeline containing overlaid information about periods of world conflict, seasonal misgivings, particular relationships with notable influencers, as well as inventions and innovative contributors of the time - the very things that shaped and molded your family's art into the refined success it is now. This customer is extremely engaged throughout your explanations and you notice a backpack decorated with countless souvenir pins collected while traveling. There's so much common ground it's hard to hold back the excitement. Your customer opens up. "I've been collecting these pins ever since the kids were old enough to travel. I'm hoping to give them rich cultural experiences from around the world that they will long remember." History? Culture? Family recipe? Your golden sock stands before you! What box will you check off next?

There's a wall containing the grand menu items and corresponding descriptions. There's something special about each and every one of your beautiful creations. What about your competitors? Well, you don't compete on the quantity of flavors you carry anymore. You'll not find Cookies n' Cream on the menu anymore, it's all about pure French magic. Utter bliss! Magnifique! Concoctions that you've personally developed from the craft as it was passed down to you, complemented by your own personal flair. With names such as Pluie d'Automne (Autumn Rain) and Froid d'Hiver (Winter's Chill) you've generated the "dream" list and each description explains the ingredients, purpose for its creation, what historical and seasonal event most influenced it, the best time of day to enjoy it, as well as a recommended drink pairing to complete the experience. You offer a choice of imported beverages that guests can buy to complement whatever creation suits their mood. Your products are sold at five times the old price. Your birds of a feather see the value of the experience as more than worth it. You are now running a money-making operation and serving a community of people all the while. Strong roots, check!

The next wall over showcases an original vintage hand cranked ice cream maker. It displays your company name and customers can take a picture as they try their hand at moving the crank. Next to the register as they purchase your products, is an illustration of your second location, opening soon. Perfection! Your Zen Dream, check! Oh my gosh, you think, this whole Zen thing is working! That eccentric author might know what he's talking about after all.

But hold on, a new visitor enters and asks, "Do you guys have Cookies 'n Cream?" Oh, that hurts! Remember to breathe. You know what to do - stomp the lukewarm movie goer out quickly with the line, "I'm sorry we don't. We specialize in the best seasonal French Vanilla you'll ever have. But If you're looking for that particular flavor, I would recommend Bob's Creamery down the street." You point the person to the direction of the shop and they follow it right out the door. There's no defeat in losing a customer that doesn't fit Your Zen Pairing. You can rejoice with this triumph. But it's time to move on because the moment of truth is at hand. That special customer who was called to your creamery takes a bite of the smooth decadence and falls into a trance of nostalgia and bliss. "This is amazing, It's feels like the countryside in the fall season. I love it!" Your Zen Phenomenon, check!

Your guest finishes with a smile, grabs one of your vintage ice-cream serving bowls and says, "Thank you so much for creating this space! I love it here. Please, include this with the sale as well! It's gorgeous!" With that you grab a special scarf with your family crest and logo on it. Hand it over and say. "I want you to have this! It's a replica of my Great Grandma's original keepsake. We are so glad you came in today." Your Zen Pounce, check!

Congratulations! Bells and whistles! You've turned a personal passion and drive into a profitable organization serving a community of people with a trail of supporters to follow. Take a moment to bask in your Zen Glory. Not too long ago you would have been offering an unexciting ice cream inventory from an uninspired supplier only to hear the words, "It's good, thanks." But now look at you, creating something no one else has - a bigger better version of your offering that no competitor can touch.

And obviously, you would annihilate Bob's Creamery when it comes to French Vanilla. This might be satisfying, but put the competitive mindset on hold for a moment. This is the world of Zen. There's no such thing as competition on the Zen Side of Business Ownership. The universe has a special place just for you. Thank goodness, you've finally taken your seat. It should be obvious now, nobody is vying for a spot that only you can fill with Your Zenersity, skillsets, passions and dreams. So enjoy your success. You've earned it.

What about Bob's Creamery? What's been going on all this time? You've been far too busy on your own enterprise to even begin to wonder about the rest of the marketplace. How nice. You haven't had an ounce of time to peer over to take a peek. Are they still the big kid on the block? Could Bob's still be a thorn in your side? Who cares, right? But consider, in the not too distant past, you would have parked out front to scope things out. Curious as to who was driving in and how many customers they were getting per hour just short of redirecting their patrons over to your creamery. But you don't have time for that now with all the growth meetings and planning on your plate. So out of curiosity, maybe it's time to do a little checking.

A quick glimpse of the establishment reveals the latest news. Something hits you smack dab in the face. Their building displays a banner that throws you back in your chair. What on earth? Bob's is offering a Wednesday special - "Half off on French Vanilla!" Is this for real? You laugh out loud. Is Bob's now trying to keep up with you? If Bob's sees your offering as a threat, that can only mean one thing for their organization and it doesn't include the word Zen. It feels good to be on this side of Zen doesn't it? While the old you may have felt threatened by the whole thing, now you secretly smile, look around at your magnificent creation of a business, flick off the lights as you lock up, and think to yourself, "Good luck with that, Bob's."

Chapter Take Aways

Your Zen Pairing; Finding the perfect customers who are engaged and invested in Your Zen Offering is vital to your Zen equation. By careful customer vetting and the establishment of your own distinct target market, rather than focusing on your competition's approach will create a customer base who become not only repeat customers, but also solid promoters of your business. Reflecting on the special moments in your history as a business owner will guide you to finding those who are the best match for your business. Ranking them and applying Your Zen Tap to attract them will transport you directly to the Zen Side of Business Ownership.

LEAVE A LEGACY

YOU'VE EARNED YOUR TITLE. DISPLAY IT PROUDLY!

Congratulations! You are well on your way to super stardom, to make your mark on this planet forever. It's time to take the training wheels off, but I have one final anecdote to test if you are ready for the open road.

A friend has recommended that you try a new location for lunch, a quirky hole in the wall. Apparently, they serve up the best pastrami sandwich you'll ever have. When you ask for the name of the restaurant, your friend replies, "Oh, its that place on the corner." With the street intersections and general vicinity located, you quickly look up the establishment. Search after search, page after page you can find nothing. So you hop in the car and head down to the corner.

As you pull up you see a tiny sign that says "Sandwiches" right above the door. No wonder this place was impossible to find online. You park in front and walk in. This has to be it. You look around. Tempting photos of menu items adorn the walls and you spot what you came for, a hefty pastrami sandwich. The place is actually called "Delectable Tom's" and they have an amazing triple layer pastrami sandwich. You enjoy it with delight and tell your friend that the meal has successfully made its way to your stomach.

What is amiss with this scenario? The product was great. The offering was unique. Patterning was evident. The staff even yelled "One pastrami coming up!" So all is well, right?

Have you ever had such an experience? Walking up to an establishment, possibly meeting the owner and being blown away by the product only to find out the location has no identifying signage? This is one of the worst betrayals imaginable complete with financial tragedy written all over it. It is also perhaps one of the most overlooked details in a business undertaking. This is serious stuff. Although it may not be evident at first glance, the repercussions of this betrayal will do you in without any sign or warning. So I'll ask another million-dollar question to help you steer clear from the doom ahead and create an organization that truly embodies you - Zen Element #1.

MOVEMENT 13: YOUR ZEN TITLE

Do you have a name? Of course you do! Your name is Person Holding Book. Right? I will now refer to you as Person Holding Book. What? Is something wrong? By all accounts you are in fact, a person holding the book. So shouldn't your name be Person Holding Book. It seems perfectly logical. Did you really think you had a name? The excuses for our opening anecdotal tragedy are as countless as the grains of sand on a beach. Everything from, "Oh, that sign is old." Or "I wanted people to know what we make." Or "Our name is this but we mostly sell that." have been used throughout time.

You have a legacy and a responsibility to make a mark in your community. You have locations to add, pallets of widgets yet to sell, and tens of thousands of followers to serve. All those systems and products you create are your ticket to success, a unique formula for the perfect customer experience, your way. Everything needs a fitting name, something that your followers can point to and remember for all time.

Wherever you are on your business journey, it has no doubt taken a massive effort to get there. You took the road less traveled. As an explorer trudging through uncharted territory to the finish line, you are using your passions to move forward. Just like an explorer, you will mark every one of your milestones with a tag. Everything from your systems, to your products, and even your company must have a name - Your Zen Title. From this day forward none of them will ever go unnoticed. Your customers will know them. Do you really want to be known as Person Holding Book? I imagine not. You are a unique individual with years of experience under your belt relying on learning moments that no one else could begin to understand.

Countless fortunes and numerous learning experiences have molded you into the beautiful person you've become. You have a name.

A very unrewarding feeling is that of being mistaken for a cog. A nameless faceless sprocket employed to yield another person's particular demands. A gear in the world of suppliers for whatever craft you do well. Wouldn't you say that it's time to look at Your Zen Title with the utmost attention?

You have a name, so it's time to start using it. This is not a lesson about sign making; you will never be just the place on the corner. It may be a cultural choice to have only locals know your menu items, a sort of rite of passage for your loyal supporters. Your Zen Pounce. I'm in your corner on this one. Especially when it comes to expressing yourself and your business in unique ways. But your execution must be impeccable. You must plan how it all goes down. The seamless experiences are those that take the most effort. If you're really going to play the anti-brand card, then take it all the way. Be sure never to hand out a business card let alone have one.

For most of us, when we make somebody's day brighter from hard work, we want to be sure to cash in on it all. Your customer must know who created the experience and what to call it. These weeks of Zen planning, patterning, pouncing, dreaming, pairing and much more are sure to make your customers dance with delight. They must know who made them happy, who to thank, who left them speechless with a Zen Phenomenon like no other. This last lesson is aimed at making sure your patrons know your company name. Your business card will have your title, your door will have your title, your systems will have your title and your products will have your title. Your everything will have your title.

Creating something that is truly unique in this world is your job. You've worked diligently through Your Zen Code to help guide your new systems and products. Give corresponding names to these. Do not be shy about it. You've been graced with the desire to be something bigger than yourself, to create new inventions. Don't betray those creations by downplaying them as ordinary. Give your invention a name that is as unique as the creation itself. If you named your bakery Decadence Heaven, then that's who you are. You are not "Cupcakes Here." You are not "Sweets Sold Here." You are not "Cakes For Sale." The sign on your street must say Decadence Heaven.

You run a jewelry store by the name of Sarah's Boutique. You have several product lines, each one with a corresponding title. How will your customer know your products? How will they identify it when they return to show a friend? Everything needs a name.

"Here is one of our most popular necklaces. It is called *Summers Reflection* from our *Princess Line*. Would you like to try it on? As a reminder, when you purchase a *Princess Line* item, Sarah's Boutique will include a polishing service as a courtesy." Do you see the difference? You are not "Sandwiches." You are not "that place on the corner." You are Delectable Tom's. And you have a *Triple Layer Pastrami Bonanza*!

Are these naming convention exercises just a fancy way to get you to brand or enforce intellectual property practices? In some respects, yes. But Your Zen Title is much more than just another item on your to-do list. Your Zen Title proclaims to the world of commerce your offering in a way that your following of supporters can get behind. It has less to do with legalese or reinforcement marketing and everything to do with building a legacy. Look for ways to solidify your creations in whatever form fits your fancy. In some cases, trademarking and seeking legal counsel would be in order. More importantly, Your Zen Titles are an extension of Your Zen Code, of you. Create them, use them, and refer to them. Start giving your followers something to take away.

Putting yourself out there means having to face the harsh world of opinions and feedback from your customers. But let's make one thing clear, Your Zen Titles should be music to your ears. This isn't a contest of how fast you can produce names and sacrifice ever-important quality. It's about staying true to what you stand for and what you have created. Like every one of your Zen Movements, this takes time to accomplish. Storyboard your list of candidates until something resonates with the core of your offering and ultimately, you.

Per the Zen world, when inspiration strikes, it's usually for the better. Just like all things worthwhile, putting a name to your methods and practices will require development hours. How many products do you offer? How many patterns have you created? Design a priorities list starting with your guiding compass - Your Zen Code. What name would you call it? You could refer to it as your "code", but that isn't searching deep enough. Don't be normal. Name it something special. Take a good look at the name of your enterprise and trusted offerings. Address them. Do the names truly embody who you are and what you do? Maybe there's a change in the works.

In many cases, the gap between where you are and where you want to be will warrant some fine-tuning. This doesn't mean you should throw everything in the trash and start over if you aren't happy with the current state of your titling. This is not an exercise to take you out of your element or have you perform an incredible amount of additional work. You have a business to run. You only need to address that which makes sense logistically and fundamentally and that which does not embody you.

There is something you should understand about the importance of this drill. You will not have performed painstakingly long hours of work creating and mastering all of your Zen Movements only to simply fit in. This is all about being a shining light, a path maker, a trailblazer. It's about building courage through belief in yourself for your customers to share. Who is the best person to change your industry and show the world how it's done? You. If your company name doesn't reflect what you stand for, then perhaps a change is in order. Now might be the time to think about changing that title to something that accurately reflects who you are now.

Stop and think about some of our most influential Fortune 500 leaders and what they are known for. Did they make their name in a specific category such as food and beverage sales, retail or technology? For every one of those categories you know the corresponding title of your favorites. What sandwich? What drink of choice? Which cell phone? There's no doubt it has a name. We all have preferences and when we, as consumers, collectively speak about what we like, we use those titles to refer to our experiences with them. This is how you will know if you are on track with Your Zen Titling. Customers will begin to address these items by their title, instead of "that one over there". You'll start hearing things such as, "Please show me *Summer's Reflection*!" Or "I'll take the *Triple Layer Pastrami Bonanza*." It will be triple music to your ears.

Names take time to perfect. Continue to finesse and refine them until you hit the target, because those titles are your differentiators. Use them. Market them. Let your customers know that when they do business with you, they are getting years of proprietary engineering in every part of the creation they are purchasing from you. That is your competitive edge. Lean on Your Zen Title to ensure the legacy you've worked so hard to achieve will live on!

Exercise 8A

Spread your Zen Movements over your desk. Every

piece of the hard work you've done since you opened this book; place it all before you. It's time to give each the fitting name. Take one last holistic view of the hard work you've created. Now ask yourself a final million-dollar question. What name will you give each of your Zen creations to best embody it as you share it with your patrons, your staff, and most importantly, you? What names will drive the excitement level to outer space? Does Your Zen Offering have a name? Or rather, do the products or services you offer have a fitting titles to communicate to your customers? How about Zen Code Axiom #2 on your finished product? Does that product have a title? Does Your Zen Phenomenon strategy have a title? Give it one. Have you defined at least one of Your Zen Ways? Give it a name. What's your name for Your Zen Pattern? Finally, is your company fitted with a title that you can stand behind?

Don't stop here. What else do you feel drawn to name in your business? Take this lesson as far as your imagination will go. Write titles down and start using them. This is your chance to put a name to the efforts that you've labored over so diligently. Get it out there and be remembered for all time.

Use this list to get started.

1. What will you call Your Zen Offering?
2. What name will you give your finished products? (Zen Code#2)
3. What will you call Your Zen Phenomenon?

4. Create a name for at least one of Your Zen Ways.
5. Create a name for at least one of Your Zen Patterns
6. What is your company name? Does it need some addressing?
7. What else would you like to name?

Your Zen Flight Check Sheet

As we near the end of the final chapter, this is where we will part ways. I extend my sincerest congratulations for what you have accomplished. You've successfully completed the journey, searched within, and taken the time to do the exercises. I'm certainly grateful to have had the privilege to share it all with you. It's time to lift off. You are ready and I'm commanding you to pull the throttle and go for it. Get out of your chair, get into your Zen space and hit the launch button with all your might.

You are one of the chosen, one of the few who will step out and do something different. Of all those in the world ready to make the leap, you are closest to the edge of the water. I'm pushing you in. The floaties are off and it's time to start swimming. You have the tools. You have the mindset. And most importantly, you have yourself. You know thyself. You are not the same person who picked up this book. You are poised for the highest levels of success. You have been rebuilt, retrained, redirected to achieve stratospheric heights. Pushing on the heels of the best CEOs of our time. Don't believe me?

If you still feel compelled to think that a successful business undertaking is a matter of formulaic proven strategy you would be correct. I support that viewpoint in its entirety. That's what this journey was all about. How is this? Isn't this book supposed to be a departure from the norm? A new perspective on how to break away from what everyone else is doing? A strategy to empower the unique you, the owner and creator of the organization you've worked so hard to build? Yes, but intertwined within the structure of this guide is the perfect foundation from top to bottom in proven formulaic manner, a scalable layout of building your enterprise just like the pros. The Fortune 500 companies with strong foundations and successful growth strategies. You can see this for yourself in my last parting gift: Your Zen Flight Check Sheet.

Take command of these monumental feats you've accomplished on your journey to the Zen Side of Business Ownership. Everything is now laid out for you in perfect formulaic manner. Textbook perfect. By completing the drills, you've been guided to implement these processes into your organization. That is the key. Implementation. It is not about holding an effective tool in your hand; it's about wielding it. That is a million-dollar talent. Billion-dollar talent. You are a Zen Machine. With full integration of the most powerful business tools ready for your deployment, you can summon any one of them at the snap of a finger.

I've spent countless hours listening to a wide range of concepts and opinions about marketing, forecasting, streamlining and culture; days researching the slew of expert business teachers and speculators that have created the perfect set formula. I've heeded advice from those who seem to have the answers and amounted piles of stress from the endless list of do's and don'ts. I've crashed and burned many times throughout my career trying to follow accepted practices. I experienced years of trial, error, and discovery so that you don't have to. The small business failing statistic stops here and now with you.

Armed with the perfect integration of the most powerful ethical practices, you will now be operating from a place many companies only hope to achieve. For underneath the maze of drills and questions is the foundation for a business that will withstand the test of time. Every aspect of you and your business is aimed perfectly at the very definition of operating from the Zen Side of Business Ownership. The highest tier of exchange where your business creation embodies you, affords prosperity, brings the right people into your life and serves a community of people with your product or service. You must continue to live it. None of this Zen work is worth a single penny to you or the world unless you continually share your business expression with those around you. Your sole responsibility is to be an illuminating light for others. You must be everything you can. It's time to serve a community of people. The world needs you. Captain Connect has been summoned. You have the ability to transform the marketplace from the inside out.

You picked up this book for a reason. It is important

that you fulfill the role that you set out to create. We are on this planet creating our commerce for a comparatively short time. You must move the bar of innovation and unique expression. It is your responsibility to take your industry forward and leave a mark on the global community. You are no different than the guy next to you, or a Fortune 500 CEO. It all comes down to a question of action - whether or not you decide to get out of the comfort zone, put the pieces in place to create something bigger than you. Be an inspirational shining star. Nothing would make me happier than to see a marketplace with a rich diversity that is as unique as the individuals running it. Imagine what a terrific world that would be, one filled with endless options and creations. That's a future worth working towards. It all starts with you listening to the little voice within and following it.

Only you can keep your vision alive. You are the leader. You have the gift and talents to conquer the challenges that lie ahead. You need to help those around you to do the same. Be a teacher. Be a motivator. Remind others that they have the power within themselves to make their life whatever they dream up. Lead by example. By working hard towards your goals, you encourage others to equally work hard. You are a trailblazer and you can make this world a better place.

How do you do that? Employ Your Zen Code, Your Zen Pillar of Focus, Your Zen Pounce. Become who you were meant to be. Reach for the stars. Leave a trail where there is no foreseeable path. Push through and grow with every last bit of Zenersity you've got. Who knows, perhaps one day you may find yourself sitting across from a young business owner who is looking for words of wisdom. Show the way. Remind your protégé that at the core of a desire to run a successful business is the inherent drive to discover one's self and share every part of it with the world.

You can do this. I have and it was one of the most exciting, scary, tear jerking and exhilarating experiences ever. When you decide to follow through with the transformations set before you, you are all the better for the thought and knowledge that have gone into creating them. Don't look back. Charge forward!

I think it is time to celebrate. How about a big bowl of French Vanilla ice cream (Cookies and Cream if you prefer) or maybe a delicious green tea cocktail on a beautiful beach at sunset enjoying the peace and serenity around you? You have proudly made it to the Zen Side of Business Ownership, you deserve to honor your accomplishments in your own Zen way!

Chapter Take Aways

Your Zen Title; The right name, Your Zen Title, is a vital component of solidifying your company's future. You need to get it right for all aspects of your creation, in essence you are branding and creating a marketable and memorable name for your offering. Take the time to think about how best Your Zen Titles represent all that is you.

· · ·

Be A Shining Star. Now that you have completed the book and the exercises, you have found yourself on the Zen Side of Business Ownership. Not many reside here with you and as you do, perhaps now is the time to share what you have learned with others. Employing all you have learned through careful and creative thought will benefit not only your business, but others with whom you share your success. Lead on and invite others to join you on the journey.

ZEN FLIGHT CHECK SHEET

UNDERSTANDING THE GREATER IMPACT YOU HAVE IN THE
MARKETPLACE.

CHAPTER 1 - BE A PART OF THE WHOLE

The marketplace has been waiting for you.

Movement 1: Your Zenersity

- Establishing your niche
- Establishing your value added

Movement 2: Your Zen Offering

- Creating a sustainable value proposition
- Establishing your creative "spin"
- Translating passion within your business
- Creating your Mission Statement

CHAPTER 2 - FIND YOUR ESSENCE

You stand for something. Discover it!

Movement 3: Your Zen Code

- Creating your core values
- Creating performance metrics (customer, employees, company)
- Defining your customer promise
- Creating a baseline for culture
- Successful growth opportunities spotting

CHAPTER 3 - CREATE YOUR SPACE

Scaling your heaven on earth means putting more of you in it.

Movement 4: Your Zen Way

- Establishing systems
- Establishing consistency

Movement 5: Your Zen Pattern

- Addressing standardization

Movement 6: Your Zen Reflection

- Establishing culture
- Creating your brand identity

CHAPTER 4 - LEAD YOUR GROWTH

A clean mental slate A clean mental slate (or plate) makes all the difference.

Movement 7: Your Zen Pillar of Focus

- Understanding your leadership role
- Addressing administrative responsibilities
- Systematic problem-solving techniques
- Finessing your vision

CHAPTER 5 - INITIATE CONTACT

It's time to be the superhero you were meant to be.

Movement 8: Your Zen Tap

- Establishing your target market
- Marketing and customer connection

Movement 9: Your Zen Pounce

- Securing repeat business
- Encouraging referral business

CHAPTER 6 - BUILD STRONG ROOTS

Steady growth comes at a cost. Is your customer prepared to pay it?

Movement 10: Your Zen Dream

- Securing and planning future growth
- Pricing your product
- Creating performance metrics (customer, employees, company)

Movement 11: Your Zen Phenomenon

- Over-delivering to your customer
- Securing repeat business
- Creating "promoter" customers

CHAPTER 7 - PERFECT YOUR OFFERING

More importantly, perfect your customer.

Movement 12: Your Zen Pairing

- Creating effective customer vetting techniques
- Establishing your target market
- Creating "promoter" customers

CHAPTER 8 - LEAVE A LEGACY

You've earned your title. Display it proudly!

Movement 13: Your Zen Title

- Solidifying your company's legacy
- Establishing your brand
- Creating a marketable offering
- Inspiring other business owners

ZEN EXERCISES REVIEW

CHAPTER 1 - BE A PART OF THE WHOLE

The marketplace has been waiting for you.

Movement 1: Your Zenersity

Exercise 1A

Write down the very personality traits that define you. Your Ideologies, Proficiencies, Ethics, Influences, Eccentricities and Service oriented qualities. List three qualities for each question.

1. **1. Ideologies:** What viewpoints or ways of performing activities are unique to you?
2. **Proficiencies:** What qualities demonstrate your

aptitudes and ability to accomplish the things
you set out to do?

3. **Ethics:** What are your qualities that demonstrate
   trustworthiness? What shows your ability to
   keep a promise?

4. **Influences:** Who or what things are most
   influential to your character?

5. **Outward Eccentricities (Style):** What are the
   personal touches or ways of outwardly
   expressing yourself that define you?

6. **Service Characteristics:** How do you show the
   world or those around you that you care?

Movement 2: Your Zen Offering

Exercise 1B

$(C^Z = YZO)$ - Uncover Your Zen Offering. Fill in the
blanks on the following statement:

> **You will be the first in your industry to combine _
> (C)_ raised to new levels of _ (^{Z})_ and/to create _
> (YZO)_ for your customers.**

CHAPTER 2 - FIND YOUR ESSENCE
You stand for something. Discover it!

Movement 3: Your Zen Code

Exercise 2A

To begin to understand yourself, address the following questions.

1. What is the philosophy, or "take" you want to be known for?
2. Per your philosophy in question 1 above, how will you define a finished product?
3. What singular promise will you make to ensure that you hit your finished product from question 2 above.
4. What resources will you consult when problem solving to uphold your singular promise from question 3 above.
5. What is your signature flair?
6. How will you inspire the larger community you call the world?

Exercise 2B

Uncover your new Zen Code: Fill in your answers from 2A into the corresponding spaces.

Zen Code Axiom # 1

The reason for continually creating this business enterprise is *(Insert 2A.1)*.

Zen Code Axiom # 2

Every part of my being, organization, and staff is directed to *(Insert 2A.2)*.

Zen Code Axiom # 3

For every sale that travels through my enterprise, above all else, I will uphold the following commitment *(Insert 2A.3)*.

Zen Code Axiom # 4

In the interest of keeping my customer promise, I will always retreat to *(Insert 2A.4)* to be the guiding light for crossroad decisions.

Zen Code Axiom # 5

I will employ and ensure that my environment always embodies *(Insert 2A.5)* as a defining component and identity to which my company, staff, contractors, and other partners will universally uphold.

Zen Code Axiom # 6

My organization imbues the world with *(Insert 2A.6)*.

CHAPTER 3 - CREATE YOUR SPACE
Scaling your heaven on earth means putting "you" in it.

Movement 4: Your Zen Way

Exercise 3A.1

Make a list of all the simple routines you perform in your day taking note of your unique mannerisms. Note especially how you negotiate small tasks. Begin documenting them using whatever format that speaks to you. Example: How do you take out the trash? How do you unfold bags? What color bags? How do you place a poster on the wall? Why?

Exercise 3A.2

Disseminate this information to your team in whatever way speaks to you. Example: Write a song and sing it. Hold policy change meetings. Place informative posters on the walls and take your staff for a tour; Turn your space into a museum and be a personal tour guide.

Movement 5: Your Zen Pattern

Exercise 3B

Take a photo and start notating placements of items. What is your office pattern layout? What are your operational pattern layouts? Break patterns down into the categories of communicative, productive, and preparative. Include your team and be sure to integrate your vision during the collaborative process. Example: What is your uniform way of taking notes? Where in the office would you place them? Etc.

Movement 6: Your Zen Reflection

Exercise 3C

Using the following list of inspirations, choose one or more items that best complement your six Zen Code Axioms and find Your Zen Reflection.

> **Inspirations:** Artist, style of art, musician, band, genre of music, author, country, culture, language; leaders, scientist, philanthropists, quotes, other

Zen Code Axiom #1 – Your Philosophy of "Take"

a) Choose your inspiration(s)

b) Determine how the attribute embodies your Axiom 1?

c) Decide how / where to integrate this into your work environment.

Zen Code Axiom # 2 – The definition of your finished product or service

a) Choose your inspiration(s)

b) Determine how the attribute embodies your Axiom 2?

c) Decide how / where to integrate this into your work environment

Zen Code Axiom #3 – Your singular promise to the customer

a) Choose your inspiration(s)

b) Determine how the attribute embodies your Axiom 3?

c) Decide how / where to integrate this into your work environment

Zen Code Axiom #4 – Resources you will consult when problem solving.

a) Choose your inspiration(s)

b) Determine how the attribute embodies your Axiom 4?

c) Decide how / where to integrate this into your work environment

Zen Code Axiom #5 – Your signature flair

a) Choose your inspiration(s)

b) Determine how the attribute embodies your Axiom 5?

c) Decide how / where to integrate this into your work environment

Zen Code Axiom #6 – Your inspiration to the world
a) Choose your inspiration(s)
b) Determine how the attribute embodies your Axiom 6?
c) Decide how / where to integrate this into your work environment

CHAPTER 4 - MIND YOUR GROWTH
A clean mental slate (or plate) makes all the difference.

Movement 7: Your Zen Pillar of Focus

Exercise 4A

When you reach a kink or upset in your day-to-day keep a cool head and make a note. Write it down in one of your four bin categories.

- **Bin #1)** Issues that compromise your embodiment or aspects of Your Zenersity.
- **Bin #2)** Issues that encroach on your profitability.
- **Bin #3)** Issues that disrupt the harmony of your loyal supporters and team.
- **Bin #4)** Issues that stifle your service to the community and customers.

Exercise 4B

Assign a time to review the bins and address your notes one by one. Decide and make it a routine. Example: Once a day; Once a week; At the end of a project.

CHAPTER 5 - INITIATE CONTACT

Time to be the superhero you were born to be.

Movement 8: Your Zen Tap

Exercise 5A

Make an effort to determine how each of Your Zen Code Axioms is important to you. Spend the time to think long and hard and be thorough. Then decide where that message will best resonate with the world. Write one or two paragraphs explaining each Zen Code and why it is important to you and how it affords the consumer a greater experience? How does it help overcome a set of unique problems? How is it revolutionary?

Exercise 5B

Take each one of your new Zen Code write-ups and decide where/how that message would best be disseminated for connection. How should you communicate it to the world?

Movement 9: Your Zen Pounce

Exercise 5C

Take a moment to reflect on what your business means for this world. What are you helping create? How would you package it as a token of thanks to evoke a state of pure connection? What creation could remind your customer that there's something bigger happening between the exchange? Write down something that reflects your values and beliefs. Make it something you can produce easily, hand over, speak, and deliver in some fashion to your customer. Example: Look to Zen Code #6 (Your Contribution) for inspiration.

CHAPTER 6 - BUILD STRONG ROOTS
Steady growth comes at a cost. Is your customer prepared to pay it?

Movement 10: Your Zen Dream

Exercise 6A

Write down what you hope to achieve in 1 year, 5 years, and in 10 years. Write down everything you need to make your future offering a reality. What assets will you acquire? What will it cost? Consider wether or not your current pricing structure supports the growth trajectory you hope to achieve.

Exercise 6B

Impart your future dreams to your customers. Write down your future goal enlightenment strategy. In what fashion will they learn about your new list of assets? Explain how their contribution will make their experience better for the years to come.

Movement 11: Your Zen Phenomenon

Exercise 6C

Determine your success measuring tool. What would bring music to your ears upon hearing from your customer after a "go" with your offering. Define and measure your ability to hit your new target.

CHAPTER 7 - PERFECT YOUR OFFERING
And more importantly, perfect your customer!

Movement 12: Your Zen Pairing

Exercise 7A

Soul search; Write down the top 10 of the fondest memories you've experienced in your field. Be specific with regards to the moments in your business ownership history that made you:

1. Come alive with passion!
2. Appreciate having the best job in the world.
3. Strive hard to reach an accomplishment.
4. See yourself as "In Your Element."

Exercise 7B

Rank your list of favorite moments from GOOD to BETTER to BEST. Make all three categories on a sheet and place your most heart wrenching story last.

Exercise 7C

7C.a) Add the word "Zen Pairings" after each of the header good; better; and best.
7C.b) Add the phrase "Customers who love" before each of your nostalgic moments from the previous list.

CHAPTER 8 - LEAVE A LEGACY
You've earned your title. Display it proudly!

Movement: Your Zen Title

Exercise 8A

Make a title for the following:

1. What will you call Your Zen Offering?
2. What name will you give your finished products? (Zen Code#2)
3. What will you call Your Zen Phenomenon?
4. Create a name for at least one of Your Zen Ways.
5. Create a name for at least one of Your Zen Patterns
6. What is your company name? Does it need some addressing?
7. What else would you like to name?

Exercise 8B

Review your Zen Flight Check Sheet and be reminded of all your progress.

YOUR 13 ZEN MOVEMENTS LISTED

YOUR MOVEMENTS AT A GLANCE

1. Your Zenersity
2. Your Zen Offering
3. Your Zen Code
4. Your Zen Way
5. Your Zen Pattern
6. Your Zen Reflection
7. Your Zen Pillar of Focus
8. Your Zen Tap
9. Your Zen Pounce
10. Your Zen Dream
11. Your Zen Phenomenon
12. Your Zen Pairing
13. Your Zen Title

APPENDIX

As noted in Chapter 6, here are a couple of my favorites…

Olympic Hopefuls Donation Directory

Team USA

Team USA Luge

Team USA Bobsled & Skeleton

United States Ski & Snowboard Foundation

USA Triathlon Foundation

ACKNOWLEDGMENTS

This book would not have happened without an immense sacrifice from my close circle. I owe you dearly. Anyone who knows me is aware that with my involvement comes the intensity of a visionary who won't stand for the status quo. Thank you to all involved who have opted in on this undertaking despite my methods and madness.

To My Editors

The final creation came together as a result of a little universal synchronicity and willingness from both my editors who served from a place of giving.

To Carrie Maldonado. You came into my life with your Human Resource expertise during some of my most challenging moments in business. Your wisdom and encouragement throughout the process helped me to better express myself through writing. I am grateful.

To Carol van Ahlers. It began on the day you decided to walk your dog past our home, listen to my life's story, and jump on board the cause. You were able to see the potential of the book and transform it all while accepting numerous impromptu texts and calls. You set aside time to let me preach from my business high horse so you could dissect my deeper character and voice. Your translating wizardry is amazing. Thank you.

To My Trusted Mentor

To Dennis Aase. One of my favorite books, "The Giving Tree", pales in comparison to the solid footing you provided throughout my early adult career. I find it difficult to express in words my appreciation for what you've done. Thank you for walking into my life, providing mentorship, and taking me in as one of your own; for teaching me how to drive a race car; for selling your car collection to send me to design college. You could have abandoned our friendship when I was young and foolish, but instead you became my first customer when I quit school to open my own business. You have never demanded anything in return. It's been a 19-year journey over a 26-year friendship. None of the experiences necessary to write this book would have occurred without you. I hope for the chance to follow your lead, give a young kid a chance, and pay your generosity forward.

To My Parents

To my Mom, Susan, thank you for creating the childhood you never had. The environment of creativity, the catchy jingles you made and sang to me, and the beautiful bedtime stories have formed me. Continually mending and consoling me through all the bicycle crashes, scrapes and bruises healed me. Most of all, you always put love into the meals you cooked along with everything you did. I'll never forget that all important guidance and have put love into every creation in my adult years.

To my Dad, Tony, I salute your service to our country. You showed me how to be a man willing to take full responsibility for my actions. You shared your talent as a brilliant mechanic, not just on the diesel trucks we worked on together, but in life. Although the toys I tore apart and modified as a kid may not share the same sentiment, my ability to dissect and problem solve in business would not have been possible without your hand.

To my in-laws Lanna, Chuck, and Doug. Being welcomed into your family and your willingness to acknowledge me as a unique creator, especially when I felt powerless, was something I will be forever grateful for. Thank you for helping your daughter, my wife, with each of our newborns and making meals at every turn. Your support for our company during challenging projects and buying us groceries when times were tough can never be repaid. Your business wisdom, advice, and love were always appreciated. I will never forget my marketing does and don'ts: promote, promote, PROMOTE!

To My Sister

To Susie, your vigilance in keeping an eye on me, steering me away from trouble, getting me to design school on time, and for helping me get my first cool job in entertainment was invaluable as I matured. Thank you. My eyes were opened the day I set foot in the world of creativity on a larger scale. With regards to getting me to school on time, I'm sorry about the speeding ticket.

To My Kids

Thank you to my kids Enzo, Niko, and Mimi - for being ever patient. Understanding my deeper calling to create this book on top of all of the business fires I had to put out when you wanted so dearly to play "tickle tag" was truly heroic. I'm so proud of your ability to be pure as well as creative, and for believing that anything is possible. In doing so, you reflected back to me the qualities I most admired in myself but had lost sight of. You inspire me to reach for the stars.

To My Wife

To my better half, PJ, there are infinite reasons for thanks. I am grateful for your willingness to start a business with me. For helping me fill out all the legal forms. Thank you for pushing me farther than I would have otherwise driven myself. For listening to every one of my silly ideas with undivided attention. Thank you for letting me reinvest our earnings back into the business. Most importantly, you have raised our family and kept everything running while I was divided during the creation of the book - maybe even before then. You did the impossible of holding things together with the limited capacity and resources afforded to you. You have always put me and the kids before yourself, that has been the greatest gift. Remember, you're a great writer, I don't care what your English teacher said!

To My Educational Academies

To Art Center College of Design, 10KSB Long Beach, and EO Accelerator, I'm grateful to have had the opportunity to be trained by some of the world's most prestigious schools. The lessons, theory, drills, and solid business practices have given me the confidence and capability to do the impossible.

To G1 Design

G1 Design has always been a space that helped me define myself, learn hard lessons, set new desires, and create unique solutions to save my hide time and again. The real world experiences I faced through the good and bad gave me the satisfaction of living life to its fullest - something I'll never regret. Thank you to all who've passed through the G1 Design doors and help me evolved into someone I could never have expected in the process. I hope you'll continue to make the journey with me.

In closing, I find it necessary to stress that taking the road less traveled is never easy. It's tough enough on the leader of the effort. It's an even harder pill to swallow for those who depend on the leader's decisions and live with the consequences. Thank you all for never giving up on me.

ABOUT THE AUTHOR

Eric Uriarte is a business owner, mentor, and author dedicated to bridging the gap between one's unique idiosyncrasies and passions with successful business practices. He is passionate about guiding those seeking deeper fulfillment to steady, predictable, and scalable growth. After running his own business for 19 years and documenting the successes and failures into his new business guide, Eric understands that owning our uniqueness is the key to long term success. The marketplace is counting on us to define ourselves and express that which only we have the capacity to do. Success will never feel fulfilling nor be sustainable in the long term unless it is a reflection of one's self down to every last policy he or she creates. In addition to his experience, Eric sharpened his business training within the Entrepreneurs Organization (EO) and is a graduate of the Goldman Sachs 10,000 small business MBA program - A scholarship intensive course distributed by the world's most prestigious organization in business leadership and training, Babson College.

You can connect with him at www.Zenersity.com